SER

HITLER'S DOMESTIC POLICY

Andrew Boxer

Collins
Educational

Published by Collins Educational
An imprint of HarperCollins*Publishers*
77–85 Fulham Palace Road
London W6 8JB

First published 1997

ISBN 0 00 327117-X

Andrew Boxer asserts the moral right to be identified as the author of this work.

British Library Cataloguing in Publication Data
A catalogue record for this book is available from the British Library.

Acknowledgements

The author and publishers would like to thank the following for permission to reproduce illustrations:

AKG London (pp. 8, 15, 20, 22, 36)

Cover photograph: Nazi poster: 'Build new youth hostels and homes'. Weimar Archive

Edited by Lorimer Poultney
Series design by Derek Lee
Picture research by Tamsin Miller
Production by Susan Cashin

Printed and bound by Scotprint Ltd, Musselburgh

Contents

1 The Nazi seizure of power, 1933–34

How were the Nazis able to seize power and establish their dictatorship so quickly?

Key points

- ◆ The destruction of the constitution
- ◆ Germany becomes a one-party state
- ◆ The threat of the 'Second Revolution'
- ◆ The purge of the SA
- ◆ Why was the seizure of power so swift?

The destruction of the constitution

At noon on Monday, 30 January 1933, President Hindenburg reluctantly appointed Adolf Hitler Chancellor (Prime Minister) of Germany. That evening NSDAP (Nazi Party) members all over Germany staged huge torchlight rallies and parades to celebrate the event and frighten their left-wing opponents. Most of the 850,000 Nazi Party members believed that everything they had campaigned and fought for would now be achieved. They expected jobs and positions of power for themselves and the chance to put Nazi ideas immediately into practice. Hitler's aims were not quite the same.

Like his party, Hitler wanted speedy political changes to establish a Nazi dictatorship, but he appeared in a weak position in January 1933. His new government was a coalition; its decrees needed the support of the President; and there were only three Nazis in a Cabinet of 12 members, many of whom disliked and distrusted one another. Hitler had accepted this arrangement because there was no other way of getting into power legally and it seemed that he could not afford to upset the conservative politicians surrounding the President.

Hitler had carefully chosen which Cabinet posts should be given to Nazis. Göring was put in charge of the police force in Prussia – a state which comprised three-fifths of Germany – while Frick, as Reich Minister of the Interior, would have some control over the rest. Hitler had also insisted on new Reichstag elections which he hoped would deliver the parliamentary majority he needed to destroy the constitution of the Weimar Republic.

The seizure of power begins

Göring carried out an immediate purge in Prussia, replacing a number of police chiefs and regional governors with SA or NSDAP bosses. On 22 February he made SA and SS (see Glossary of Terms on page 46) members in Prussia into auxiliary policemen. This legalised their violence against left-wing opponents: communists, socialists and trade unionists. Göring's example inspired SA leaders all over Germany. On their own authority, they terrorised their enemies. They destroyed offices, smashed printing presses, and set up makeshift concentration camps where thousands were imprisoned and tortured. The speed and ruthlessness of it all were startling. Indeed, the spontaneous and ill-disciplined behaviour of the rank-and-file of the Nazi Party, although it was useful in destroying the power of the left, also became embarrassing to the leadership. Hitler needed to bring his party under control.

He also knew that his power would not be complete until he had destroyed the Weimar constitution and given the Nazi seizure of power the legal gloss essential to reassure his conservative allies and the millions of respectable, middle-class Germans who had voted for him. The Reichstag Fire and the Enabling Law were important as they allowed Hitler to acquire the power he needed, not only to create his dictatorship, but also to discipline his own party.

The Reichstag Fire

On the night of 27 February, the Reichstag building went up in flames. Hitler immediately blamed the Communists and Göring ordered the mass arrest of Communist Reichstag deputies and party officials. The next day President Hindenburg was persuaded to issue an Emergency Decree suspending civil freedoms and allowing the government to imprison political opponents indefinitely. By the end of April there were as many as 25,000 people in 'protective custody' in Prussia alone.

The decree also allowed Frick, as Reich Minister of the Interior, to take over the powers of the governments of those regional states (*Länder*) which were unable to maintain law and order. To control the chaos the SA were creating everywhere, Frick used the decree to appoint reliable Nazi police chiefs in each of the states. His actions both destroyed Germany's federal system and gave the Berlin government more control over its unruly party members.

The Reichstag Election and the Enabling Law: March 1933

The Reichstag election took place on 5 March 1933. The Nazis increased their share of the vote from 33.1% in November 1932 to 43.9%. This was because many Germans, especially those in the middle classes, admired the tough action the Nazis were taking against the Communists. Furthermore, the Nazis were backed by the authority of the state and the momentum of their propaganda machine, superbly orchestrated by Joseph Goebbels.

The election gave them 288 seats (out of a total of 647) in the new parliament. However, Hitler needed a two-thirds majority to pass legislation that would destroy the constitution and establish a one-party dictatorship. With the Communist deputies arrested and some of the Socialists forbidden to take their seats, the Nazis needed only the votes of the Catholic Centre Party to secure the passage of the Enabling Law, transferring the power to make laws from the Reichstag to the Cabinet (in effect, to Hitler himself). The Centre Party was subjected to a mixture of promises and threats. Hitler publicly pledged himself to respect the rights of the Catholic Church but it was also plain that individual Catholics would be intimidated if the Party did not co-operate.

The new Reichstag was opened on 21 March at Potsdam, the seat of the old Prussian monarchy. Goebbels turned the event into a massive nationalist ceremony, designed to reassure conservatives, and Hindenburg in particular, that the Nazi seizure of power would restore traditional German values and power. Two days later, for the debate on the Enabling Law in the Kroll Opera House, the SA and SS were drawn up in large numbers to intimidate the Socialists (SPD). In the event, despite the courageous opposition of the SPD deputies, the Enabling Law was passed by 441 votes to 94.

Germany becomes a one-party state

The legal destruction of the remaining opposition to the Nazis followed swiftly, although any chance of effective resistance from the left-wing parties had already been destroyed by the Nazis' wave of terror. On 7 April laws were passed to remove political opponents and Jews from the Civil Service and the legal profession. In a bid to win working-class support for the Nazi regime, Hitler proclaimed 1 May (international labour day) an official public holiday, but on the following day detachments of the SA and SS occupied any trade union offices that had not already been destroyed. All trade unions were now merged into the German Labour Front (*Deutsche Arbeitsfront* – DAF) under the leadership of Robert Ley. On 22 June the SPD was formally outlawed.

The middle-class parties, the DDP and the DVP, had ceased to be of any significance before 1933 because they had lost most of their electoral support to the Nazis. At the end of June, each party voted to dissolve itself. Hitler's Nationalist allies in the government, the DNVP, proved equally easy to push aside. Their paramilitary organisation – the *Stahlhelm* – had joined the Nazis in April, their political leader, Alfred Hugenburg, resigned from the Cabinet on 26 June and, on the following day, the remainder of the party merged with the Nazis.

Hitler had already neutralised the Centre Party by persuading them to vote for the Enabling Law and in July his government negotiated a formal agreement with the Roman Catholic Church, known as the Concordat. This prohibited the clergy from political activity. The Catholic authorities were much more concerned about their freedom to preach and their control over Catholic schools than about preserving the political power of the Centre Party. On 5 July the Party formally dissolved itself, to be followed two days later by its Bavarian ally, the BVP. On 14 July a law proclaimed the NSDAP as 'the only political party in Germany', formally confirming what had already been established. German democracy had been destroyed in less than six months. As Goebbels wrote in his diary: 'all this had been achieved much more quickly than we had dared to hope'.

The threat of the 'Second Revolution'

On 6 July 1933 Hitler pronounced that the National Socialist revolution was over and in August the SA lost their status as auxiliary policemen. It seemed that there was no future for the SA, except as a propaganda organisation. Ernst Röhm, the leader of the SA, disagreed and so did many of his followers. In May 1933 Röhm had issued a directive which said: 'The SA and the SS have gained a victory on a barely conceivable scale, of which they may justly be proud. But before them lies the task of completing the National Socialist revolution and creating the Third Reich. It seems to me that there is still some tough work and a hard struggle before us.'

The aims of this so-called 'second revolution' were incoherent because the SA knew what they disliked but were vague about the kind of society they wanted to create. Many SA men were social misfits who disliked conventional society and wanted to sweep away the conservative, capitalist establishment. Most wanted to enjoy the power and status that Weimar Germany had denied them, and during the first six months of 1933 had eased themselves into well-paid jobs, established some local political power for themselves and terrorised concentration camp detainees. Some had even set up protection rackets. They had always disliked Hitler's insistence on obtaining power legally and were suspicious of his apparent willingness to do deals with conservative politicians, businessmen and generals.

During 1933 Röhm became increasingly critical of Hitler, and said to his friends: 'Adolf is rotten. He's betraying all of us. He only goes around with reactionaries.' Röhm was particularly annoyed because Hitler did not support his plan to make the SA into Germany's new army. He was especially contemptuous of the generals, calling them 'a bunch of old fogies who certainly aren't going to win the new war'.

Hitler's attitude towards the SA

Röhm and the SA presented Hitler with a dilemma. On the one hand, Röhm was one of his oldest friends and throughout his life Hitler remained loyal to those who had been with the Party from its earliest days: the men he called the 'old fighters'. Hitler also shared Röhm's objectives for making German society more Nazi and for purging it of racial enemies like the Jews. On the other hand, he had more tactical sense than Röhm and realised that these things could not be done in a hurry. In particular, Hitler knew that he would have to rely on the expertise of the conservative economists and professional soldiers if Nazi Germany was to be prepared for a war of revenge and conquest. The SA might be good at hitting communists over the head with chair legs, but that did not mean they could take on the armies of France or the USSR in modern battle.

Furthermore, Hitler was irritated by the independence and lawlessness of the SA. He wanted a Nazi Party totally loyal to himself. The SA's violence had been useful while political power was being won, but now it threatened Germany's fragile economic recovery. Finally, Hitler had his eye on the President. If the SA were not brought under control, the old man might be persuaded by the army generals and his conservative advisers to dismiss Hitler. To succeed Hindenburg and complete his political power by combining the offices of Chancellor and President, Hitler would need the support of the Army.

Enemies of the SA

By the beginning of 1934 the generals were alarmed about the SA. The Army, limited by the Treaty of Versailles, was only 100,000 strong, but SA numbers had grown enormously since the Nazis came to power. It is impossible to know exactly how large the SA was, but some historians claim that it had as many as 3 million members by 1934. On 1 February, Röhm, who had been made a Cabinet minister in December, proposed his scheme for merging the Army with the SA and SS. The generals were horrified. As General von Brauchitsch later remarked: 'rearmament was too serious and difficult a business to permit the participation of crooks, drunkards and homosexuals.' On 28 February

Figure 1
Ernst Röhm (centre), followed by Himmler (left).

Hitler summoned the SA and SS leaders to a meeting with the Army commanders and made it clear that the SA would not be given a military role. Röhm was not pleased and the Army leaders continued to fear that he might launch a violent coup to seize power.

The generals were not the only ones who disliked and feared Röhm. Two senior Nazi leaders, Göring and Himmler, had their own reasons for wanting to see him eliminated. Göring fancied himself as Germany's commander-in-chief and regarded Röhm as a rival. Himmler was the leader of the SS, the Nazi Party's own police force, which was subordinate to the SA. If Himmler were to achieve his ambition of making the SS into Germany's police force, he would have to break free of SA control. Göring and Himmler got together. Their aim was to accumulate enough evidence of an SA plot to seize power that Hitler would be forced to act. Evidence of SA lawlessness, corruption and homosexuality was not hard to find but there was nothing to suggest that Röhm was planning a coup. Whether Hitler seriously believed what Himmler and Göring told him remains uncertain but their 'evidence' provided him with an excuse to act when the time came.

The purge of the SA

The Marburg speech

The crisis came to a head in June when it became clear that Hindenburg did not have long to live. On 17 June the Vice-Chancellor, Franz von Papen, made a speech in Marburg criticising the SA and their demand for a 'second revolution'. He implied that Hitler was not doing enough to bring them under control. Hitler realised that Röhm would have to be dealt with quickly if the Army and the conservatives were to allow him to become President when the old man died.

The Night of the Long Knives

Röhm had sent the SA away on annual leave, which meant they were highly vulnerable when Hitler struck. In the early hours of 30 June 1934 Hitler arrived at Röhm's holiday hotel in Bad Wiessee, a resort near Munich. He ordered the immediate arrest of Röhm and some of his senior SA cronies, pretending to be shocked that one of them was discovered in bed with a young man. Meanwhile in Berlin, Göring was busy rounding up SA men on his death list. There were no trials; the victims of the purge were shot within hours of their arrest. In Munich, Röhm survived a little longer; he refused his captors' invitation to commit suicide and was shot by two SS men in his prison cell the following day. The purge included a number of people who had nothing to do with the SA as the Nazi leaders took the opportunity to settle a few old scores. Estimates of the number of victims vary; at least 83 died, but the total may have been over 200.

The army leaders, who had provided the weapons and transport for the purge, were delighted. When Hindenburg died on 2 August, Hitler combined the offices of Chancellor and President and the Army agreed to a new oath of loyalty to Hitler personally as '*Führer* of the German Reich and people'.

The significance of the purge

It was Himmler and the SS who benefited most. By breaking free of the SA and taking control of its concentration camps the SS took another big step towards becoming Germany's police force. The purge made it clear that the Nazis would not bother with the official legal system in dealing with their enemies. In future, Germans could expect the Party's police agencies to enforce the law – and there was no appeal against their decisions.

In his Reichstag speech about the purge on 13 July, Hitler said that the Army would now be 'the only bearer of arms' in the nation but he soon broke this promise by allowing the SS to carry weapons and, later, to establish military units. The Army had been the only organisation capable of opposing Hitler but, by helping with the purge, it had thrown away its independence.

Hitler's personal popularity soared after the Night of the Long Knives. Most Germans disliked the corruption and arrogance of the SA and welcomed the decisive action against it. Hindenburg's telegram to Hitler seemed to sum up their relief: 'By your determined action and gallant personal intervention . . . you have saved the German nation from serious danger. For this I express to you my most profound thanks and sincere appreciation.'

Why was the seizure of power so swift?

- **The mixture of legality and violence**. The Nazis' combination of legality and violence was the single most important reason for the speed and success of their seizure of power. Opponents found themselves squeezed between the power of the central government in Berlin and violent pressure applied from below by local Nazis. The legal destruction of the Weimar constitution made opposition into treason, reassured doubters and enabled Hitler to legalise the violent actions of his supporters.
- **Hitler's political skill**. Hitler was both single-minded and an opportunist. He knew exactly what he wanted but was flexible enough to seize opportunities (such as the Reichstag Fire) when they came up or to abandon allies (like Röhm) if necessary. He was also skilful at disguising his real aims. This allowed his rivals to think that he agreed with them.
- **The misjudgements of the conservatives.** The conservatives who had put

Hitler into power in January 1933, believing they could control him, underestimated the Nazis' capacity for ruthlessness. As a group, the conservatives shared Hitler's dislike of the democratic constitution and they were delighted to see the left-wing parties and the trade unions destroyed. They fooled themselves into thinking that Hitler had abandoned his more extreme ideas – a feeling that seemed to be confirmed by his purge of the SA.

- **The weaknesses of the opposition.** The power of the left was potentially formidable. The combined support for the communist KPD and the socialist SPD in November 1932 exceeded the Nazi vote. But the two left-wing parties could not work together. Each regarded the other as an enemy as dangerous and deadly as the Nazis. Even more damaging was the high level of unemployment caused by the depression because few workers were willing to risk their jobs by going on strike against the Nazis. Both parties were surprised how quickly and savagely they were attacked by the SA after Hitler's appointment as Chancellor. This made the organisation and mobilisation of opposition impossible. The tactics of the Socialists helped the Nazis: they decided not to do anything illegal because they did not wish to provide Hitler with an excuse to ban them. They had no answer to his methods except a courageous, but futile, vote against the Enabling Law. Apart from the left-wing parties, all other groups were anxious to make deals and agreements with the Nazis as fast as possible.
- **The absence of an alternative to Nazi dictatorship.** Germany had struggled to find a stable government since the fall of Müller's coalition government in March 1930. Those who disliked the Nazis were unable to find an alternative leader able to mobilise popular support. Only the SPD wanted to preserve the Republic. Even the KPD were happy to see it destroyed because they believed that its fall would be followed by the triumph of communism. By the time they realised their mistake, they were behind bars.

Studying 'The Nazi seizure of power'

1. Make sure you understand the sequence of events between January 1933 and August 1934. Construct a timeline that includes all the key events mentioned in this chapter.
2. It is important to be able to identify the separate reasons for the Nazis' success. Make notes on the following themes and place them in order of importance: the role of terror; the legal powers acquired by Hitler; Hitler's political skill; the weaknesses of the Nazis' opponents; the groups and individuals who were prepared to help the Nazis.
3. The Night of the Long Knives was a crucial event. Use the following headings to structure your notes on it:
   - why the SA wanted an immediate 'second revolution'
   - why Hitler did not
   - the role played in the build-up to the purge by: Himmler, Göring, von Papen, the generals
   - the events of the purge
   - the significance of the purge.

2 Imposing Nazi doctrine

The police state, culture, education and women

Key points

- How was the Third Reich governed?
- The growth of SS power
- Cultural conformity
- Youth and education
- Nazi policy towards women

How was the Third Reich governed?

Hitler governed Germany in the same way as he had led the Nazi Party before he became Chancellor. He was the all-powerful *Führer* whose word was law. This did not mean that he was responsible for all decisions in the Third Reich or even that he initiated all policies – far from it – but it did mean that his decisions could override all laws, rights and systems. As one of his lawyers said: 'the position of *Führer* combines in itself all sovereign power of the Reich . . . political power is given to the *Führer* as the executor of the nation's common will.'

How far Hitler was personally responsible for policy decisions in the Third Reich is a matter of some debate among historians although it is clear from his daily routine and lifestyle that he was content to leave much of the day-to-day business of government to his subordinates. Hitler disliked Berlin, was bored by paperwork and refused to take on the task of co-ordinating government policy. As one of his aides observed, 'he took the view that many things sorted themselves out on their own if one did not interfere'. Hitler did play a major role in the two areas which he regarded as the true business of great statesmen – foreign policy and war – and he intervened decisively in other areas of policy when he felt the need. He was also critically important in establishing the tone and direction of Nazi policy. No major initiatives were possible without his backing and no individuals or agencies could gain power without his support.

As leader of the Nazi Party Hitler had allowed his subordinates considerable freedom to make their own decisions and to interpret Nazi policy, provided they had shown unswerving loyalty to him. He maintained this practice in government. His style was summed up by a government official in 1934: 'Everyone who has the opportunity to observe it knows that the *Führer* can hardly dictate from above everything which he intends to realise sooner or later . . . It is the duty of everybody to try to work towards the *Führer* along the lines he would wish. Anyone who makes mistakes will notice it soon enough.'

Nazi government in practice

Because Hitler did not co-ordinate the policies of his ministers, refused to let anyone else do so and allowed individuals considerable freedom to initiate policies, the government of the Third Reich soon became a jungle of competing centres of power. This was made worse by the failure of attempts to define the role of the Nazi Party after 1933. Hitler had no intention of destroying the existing government ministries and even added four new ones. But he also allowed Party members to set up agencies, some of which grew sufficiently powerful to challenge and even destroy the authority of ministries. The best example of this is the SS, which became the police authority in Germany and effectively neutered the Ministry of the Interior.

Ambitious Party men secured for themselves government posts as well as Party positions. Walther Darré, for example, combined the role of Party agrarian boss with that of Minister of Agriculture. Many of the Party's regional leaders – the *Gauleiters* – were quick to seize positions of power in the localities and to build their own private empires. Erich Koch, the *Gauleiter* of East Prussia, made himself the senior administrative official there and monopolised power so successfully that he even kept the SS at bay. Hitler added to the confusion by creating special agencies to carry out particular tasks. For example, in 1933 he made Fritz Todt Inspector-General of the German Road and Highway System. Armed with Hitler's personal authority, Todt was able to cut across government departments and Party agencies to build a personal empire that controlled waterways, power plants and even the building of Germany's Western Wall defences in occupied France during the war.

The most powerful barons in Nazi Germany were those who successfully 'worked towards the *Führer*' by anticipating and executing Hitler's will. They were also ruthless in cutting down rivals. Göring, who came to dominate the German economy, and Himmler, as leader of the SS, are two prominent examples. There were also failures. Alfred Rosenberg and Walther Funk, despite holding impressive titles, wielded little power because they lacked the necessary personal authority and political cunning.

Not surprisingly, Hitler's method of government was inefficient. It was a system in which power was awarded to individuals rather than to offices, so it offered plenty of scope for corruption and gave individuals and agencies a vested interest in competing with one another rather than co-operating. Much time, energy and money was devoted to in-fighting between rivals for power. But the system suited Hitler because he believed that the best men would emerge from the process of struggle. It also enhanced his own power because everyone needed his favour to advance their careers or beat off rivals.

Despite this, the regime was successful in achieving some of its goals, one of which was to create the impression of an efficient, disciplined society. The Third Reich mobilised the energies and expertise of many Germans and achieved a number of much-vaunted successes in economic and foreign policy in the 1930s. How real those successes were and whether more could have been achieved requires closer examination.

The growth of SS power

The Third Reich rested on two pillars. The first was popular support, real or imagined. The second was coercion. The principal function of the SS was to create and run a police and surveillance system that was all-pervasive and ruthless. Their leader – Heinrich Himmler, the *Reichsführer* SS – had deliberately created the SS as an élite, fanatically devoted to Hitler and the ideas of Nazism. This made it the ideal agency for carrying out in wartime the regime's most extreme policies – the systematic murder of its racial enemies.

The origins of the SS

The SS (*Schutzstaffel* – 'guard unit') was formed in 1925 as Hitler's personal bodyguard because he did not fully trust the SA. When Himmler became its leader in 1929 it comprised 280 men and was subordinate to the SA. Himmler immediately expanded it, aiming to create a corps of racially pure, dedicated Nazis who would become Germany's new aristocracy. He made the SS into the Party's own police force and gave it its distinctive black uniform with the death's head insignia. In 1932 he established the SD (*Sicherheitsdienst* – 'security service') as the intelligence service of the SS.

By the time Hitler became Chancellor, SS numbers had rocketed to 52,000. To make it into Germany's new police force Himmler had to take control of the police in each of the German states and fight off rivals such as the Minister of the Interior, Wilhelm Frick. Within a year Himmler had taken over the political police in most of the states outside Prussia and in April 1934 he took charge of the Prussian secret state police (the *Gestapo*) from Göring. The two men plotted the downfall of Röhm. The SS was rewarded for its part in the Night of the Long Knives by becoming independent of the SA and being permitted to form armed units which, early in the war, became the *Waffen*-SS.

The SS police empire

After the Röhm purge the SS took control of the concentration camps that the SA had created. In July 1934 Theodor Eicke, commandant of Dachau for a year, was appointed Inspector of Concentration Camps. Eicke had made Dachau into the model SS camp, replacing the arbitrary brutality of the SA with systematic, bureaucratically organised terror. Eicke ensured that all camps were run on his Dachau model and he trained the SS camp guards (*Totenkopfverbände* – 'Death's Head Units') to be as brutal as the system they enforced.

The *Gestapo* decided who was sent to concentration camps. Under the leadership of Himmler's deputy, Reinhard Heydrich, it expanded into a nationwide organisation to hunt down 'enemies of the state'. These included not just those guilty of specific offences but those whose racial origins or 'mentality hostile to the state' placed them outside the Nazis' idea of the 'national community'. The concepts of 'protective custody' and 'preventive arrest' were invented to justify the detention of many whose sentences had been completed or who had been acquitted by the ordinary courts.

Despite its fearsome reputation, the *Gestapo* was not particularly large. In 1939 there were only 15,500 agents to police a nation of nearly 80 million. It is clear that, for much of its surveillance work, the *Gestapo* relied on the active cooperation of the German people. This is shown by Table 3 on page 47. The *Gestapo* also supplied the leadership with some of its only reliable information on public opinion. Popular attitudes to such mundane issues as price increases and employment prospects as well as more critical questions like foreign policy were constantly monitored. This shows not just that the *Gestapo* was determined to root out opposition, but also that the regime was acutely sensitive about its popularity.

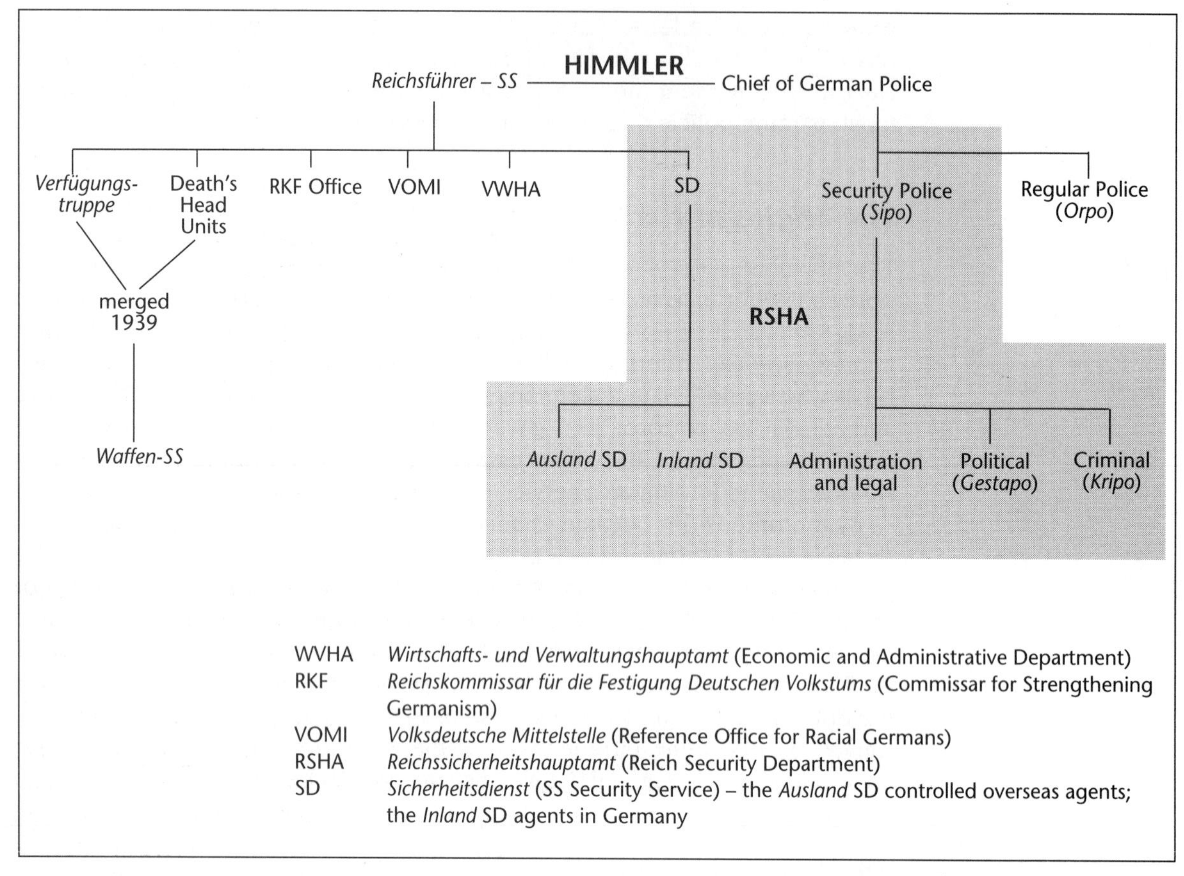

Figure 2
The structure of the SS and police system.

The expansion of the SS empire

Himmler, rather than Frick, was appointed Chief of the German Police in June 1936. He reorganised the police into two main departments, placing Heydrich in charge of the Security Police, which included the *Gestapo*. Heydrich continued as head of the SD which did similar work to the *Gestapo* and was staffed by some of the same people. It was typical of the confusion of Nazi government that the respective roles of the two organisations were never satisfactorily defined even though they were formally merged into one Reich Security Department (RSHA) in 1939.

Hitler's élite armed bodyguard were renamed the *Leibstandarte Adolf Hitler* in 1933. The *Führer*'s gratitude for their role in the SA purge enabled Himmler to expand the armed formations of the SS who, in 1934, were given the title *Verfügungstruppe* (General Service Troops). Their numbers increased as Germany rearmed and reintroduced conscription, and at the outbreak of the war, they numbered 18,000. In November 1939 they were merged with the Death's Head Units to form the *Waffen*-SS and placed under the command of the Army.

The SS also developed a number of agencies that reflected Himmler's obsession with the Nazis' racial ideas, and the network of concentration camps and labour camps became the basis of a vast SS economic empire controlling enterprises involved in quarrying, brick-making, forestry, clothing, furniture and even soft drinks. By 1939 the SS were already a state within a state (see Figure 2) and their power was to grow even greater during the war, once the Nazis had the conquered territories of the east to govern and could implement their barbarous racial policies.

Cultural conformity

Just over a month after he became Chancellor, Hitler appointed the Nazi propaganda chief, Josef Goebbels, to the Cabinet as Minister of Propaganda. Both men knew the importance of propaganda in influencing public opinion and regarded control of the media and the arts as vital in the elimination of opposition. On 10 May Goebbels approved a series of book-burning ceremonies in Berlin and other university cities. Nazi students stripped libraries and bookshops of literature they disliked and then symbolically burned it in public.

In September, Goebbels established the Reich Chamber of Culture, with departments for literature, press, radio, theatre, music and the creative arts. Membership was essential for anyone wanting to work in any of these fields, which virtually removed the need for censorship. Artists censored their own work, knowing that, if they did not, they would lose their membership. By 1939 the Nazi publishing house had bought up about two-thirds of Germany's newspapers, and the Propaganda Ministry controlled the news agencies which provided them with their information.

Germany's rich cultural life was rapidly destroyed because the Nazis regarded most modern developments as decadent and degenerate, the product of 'cultural Bolshevism' and clear evidence of the corrupting influence of Jews. In the Third Reich art had to express the Nazi values of heroism, strength, nationalism and community. Nazi architecture was grand and monumental to remind people of the power and permanence of the Reich. Sculptors favoured muscular nudes in heroic poses and painters contrived sentimental scenes of domestic cosiness and rural bliss. Theatre directors and musicians played safe by performing the classics. Nazi policies produced what one historian has called an 'all-pervading atmosphere of cultural mediocrity'.

Youth and education

Hitler believed that moulding the next generation would guarantee the future of the Reich. In *Mein Kampf* he had declared that education must give priority to 'the production of bodies physically sound to the very core. The development of intellectual ability is secondary to this.' Hitler's principles shaped the Nazis' youth and education policies.

Figure 3
Hitler Youth leader Baldur von Schirach inspects Hitler Youth members at a rally, 1938.

Age	Boys	Girls
10 to 14 years	*Deutsches Jungvolk* – DJ (*Pimpfen*) (German Young People – Cubs)	*Jungmädelbund* – JM (League of Young Girls)
14 to 18 years	*Hitler Jugend* – HJ (Hitler Youth)	*Bund Deutscher Mädel* – BDM (League of German Girls)

Figure 4
The organisation of the Hitler Youth.

The Hitler Youth

The Nazis formed their own youth movement – the Hitler Youth (*Hitler Jugend* – HJ) – in 1926. Baldur von Schirach was appointed its leader in 1931 and by the time Hitler became Chancellor it had about 50,000 members, many of whom saw it as an opportunity to break away from the authority of their parents, school or church. By the end of 1933 Schirach had succeeded in bringing under his control all other youth movements, apart from those run by Roman Catholics. The Hitler Youth Law of 1 December 1936 announced that 'all German young people, apart from being educated at home and at school, will be educated in the Hitler Youth physically, intellectually, and morally in the spirit of National Socialism to serve the nation and the community'. But membership did not become compulsory until March 1939.

The organisation of the Hitler Youth is shown in Figure 4. Enrolment in the HJ was accompanied by elaborate ceremonies and an oath of loyalty to the *Führer*. The HJ motto was: '*Führer*, command – we follow.' Its emphasis was on physical and ideological training and, in conscious preparation for war, its activities became increasingly military in character.

Its effectiveness is questionable. Many parents and teachers complained that children had been brutalised by the HJ, which suggests that its emphasis on military virtues had had some effect. A good many young people enjoyed the opportunities, such as camping and hiking, that the HJ offered. Its community values, in which class distinctions were irrelevant, were popular with recruits from poorer backgrounds, though less so with middle-class members. Conscription and labour service removed potential leaders and, once the HJ became compulsory, it lost its appeal to youngsters wanting to rebel against authority. Many found the strict regimentation and the emphasis on military drill tiresome. What the historian Detlev Peukert has called the HJ's 'almost obsessive fixation on the repression of sexuality' was possibly counter-productive. After the 1936 Nuremberg rally attended by 100,000 boys and girls aged between 15 and 18, there were 900 pregnancies. By the time the war began, many young people had joined illegal gangs in an attempt to escape the suffocating influence of the Nazis.

University education

Universities proved fairly easy to bring under control. A good many teachers and students were already enthusiastic Nazis. In 1933 non-Aryan teachers were quickly purged and many of Germany's best brains left of their own accord to escape a regime that prided itself on its contempt for intellectuals. Universities lost 15% of their staff in the first 18 months of Nazi rule. Not surprisingly, both the quality of scholarship and the numbers attending university dropped dramatically. There were approximately 89,000 students in German universities in 1933. By 1939 the number had fallen to 41,000.

Schools

The Nazis were quick to purge school teachers whom they considered racially or ideologically undesirable, the pressure coming both from government officials and the teachers' own professional body. Morale in the profession slumped quickly. The Nazis despised teachers and paid them badly. Schools were subject to constant interference by the HJ, whose members were encouraged to reject their teachers' authority. By 1938 there were 3,000 vacancies for elementary school teachers. Hitler believed that retired NCOs would make ideal replacements.

Because education was an ideological issue, the Reich Minister of Education, Bernard Rust, faced constant interference from other Nazis and was unable to prevent the schools he set up to train the regime's new élite from coming under the influence of the SS. In 1937 Hitler allowed Schirach and the head of the Labour Front, Robert Ley, to establish another set of élite schools run by the Party and therefore outside Rust's control.

Most Germans were educated in the conventional school system although the curriculum was radically altered to inculcate Nazi values. The amount of time devoted to sport was increased to 15% and the syllabuses for biology, history and German were overhauled to ensure that they stressed national greatness and Nazi racial theories. Even maths could be used to make an ideological point: one textbook asked pupils to contrast the cost of a lunatic asylum with the price of domestic houses.

Nazi policy towards women

The Nazis believed that women had been designed by nature for domesticity and motherhood. Power was monopolised by men, but women did not escape regimentation in the service of the Reich. In 1934 Gertrud Scholtz-Klink was appointed leader of the Party's two principal women's movements to mobilise women for Party work in support of men. She aimed to make the NS-*Frauenschaft* (Nazi Women's Group) into an élite organisation to undertake 'the cultural, spiritual and political education of German women'. The *Deutsches Frauenwerk* (DFW) was under the control of the NS-F and claimed a membership of about 4 million in 1938; it ran courses for women on domestic science and motherhood.

Scholtz-Klink was only partially successful in achieving her goals. Full-time housewives were not easy to enlist and, besides, encouraging women to undertake Party work conflicted with the regime's desire to keep them at home. Many women remained loyal to their church groups and others disliked being saturated by Nazi propaganda. But historian Jill Stephenson has concluded that 'if there was little positive enthusiasm on the part of women for Party activities, there was no organised opposition either'.

Women in work

The Nazis aimed to remove women from the labour force and encourage them to have more children. However, whether or not women were employed was probably much more influenced by economic conditions than by propaganda, although Nazi attitudes may well have reinforced existing trends. Men were better paid than women and so families whose prosperity increased as the economy recovered could afford to support an unpaid housewife. On the other hand, the labour shortage in agriculture and the demands of conscription on the male work force pushed many women into jobs who might otherwise have stayed at home. The number of female white-collar workers increased in the 1930s but these were mostly young women employed in low-paid, mundane clerical jobs where there was a high turnover of employees.

Women and motherhood

The decline in the birth rate had been bothering German nationalists for some time. They feared that they would soon be overrun by hordes of inferior Slavs from the east. This is why even sex became a political issue in the Third Reich. One official publication declared: 'sexual activity serves the purpose of procreation for the maintenance of the life of the nation and not the enjoyment of the individual.'

As soon as they came to power the Nazis clamped down on abortion and made it harder to obtain contraceptives. Tax concessions and welfare payments were given to fertile families and in June 1933 a marriage loan scheme was introduced. Couples received an interest-free loan of RM 600 (about four months' worth of an average worker's salary), the wife was required to give up her job and a quarter of the loan was cancelled for every child born. Propaganda constantly stressed the nobility of motherhood and in 1939 the Mother's Cross was introduced to reward mothers of large families. Party members took their duty to procreate so seriously that the wife of Hitler's private secretary, Martin Bormann, not only tolerated her husband's mistress, but suggested to him:'see to it that [she] has a child one year and I have one the next, so that you always have one woman around who is in good shape'.

The number of marriages increased, as did the birth rate (see the graph on page 46), but Nazi policies were not primarily responsible. As with employment, people made decisions about family size principally for economic reasons, but it is likely that propaganda either reinforced their decisions or had some impact in countering the disincentives to procreation.

Studying 'Imposing Nazi doctrine'

1 In what ways was Nazi government inefficient? Make sure you understand the following factors: Hitler's leadership style; the role of the Nazi Party; the creation of individual empires.

2 Why did the SS become so powerful? Use this chapter as a starting point and then do some further research on:
- Himmler's leadership
- his concept of the SS as the Nazi élite
- how he increased their numbers and expanded their role
- how the SS benefited from the purge of the SA
- protective custody, the *Gestapo* and the concentration camps
- how the SS became a 'state within a state'
- the *Waffen-SS*, their economic and racial agencies.

3 What methods did the Nazis use and how successful were they in controlling: Germany's cultural life; education and youth; women?

Nazi economic policies, 1933–39

Was Germany's economy a success or failure during the 1930s under the Nazis?

> **Key points**
>
> - Hitler's economic objectives
> - The 'New Plan' and the problems of recovery
> - The radicalisation of economic policy
> - The economy and the outbreak of war
> - Who benefited and who suffered from Nazi economic policy?
> - How successfully was Nazi management of the German economy?

Hitler's economic objectives

When the Nazis came to power in 1933 Hitler had clear economic goals but no fixed ideas about how they would be achieved. His main aim was to prepare Germany for war. This meant more than just producing weapons; it required the creation of a 'defence economy' (*Wehrwirtschaft*) in which the nation's entire resources would be mobilised for a war of imperial conquest. This involved persuading the German people to accept the need for war, training Germany's youth to become good National Socialists and purging German society of people opposed to war.

Hitler's thinking about the economy had been strongly influenced by Germany's experience of the First World War. Like most Germans with right-wing views, he was convinced that the Army had not been defeated on the battlefield in 1918 but had been denied victory by the collapse of civilian morale at home. Socialist and communist agitators, he believed, had encouraged strikes and mutinies in order to destroy the effectiveness of Germany's armed forces and gain power themselves.

From this, he drew a number of lessons. Firstly, the German people must enter the next war united behind their *Führer*. For this it was essential to prepare the nation ideologically, psychologically and spiritually as well as economically. Secondly, the German economy must not be ruined by a British naval blockade. Germany must use the years of peace to become as self-sufficient as possible and reduce her dependence on overseas trade. Finally, the regime must do everything possible to maintain the living standards, and thus the morale, of the German people.

These tasks could not be completed all at once. When he came to power in January 1933, Hitler had to deal with the immediate problems caused by the Depression, which had affected Germany very severely.

The first priority: reducing unemployment

Hitler was well aware that Germany's economic difficulties had played a major part in destroying the Weimar Republic. He would have to deal with them quickly if his regime was to survive. The most obvious problem was the level of unemployment, which stood at 6 million people.

On 16 March 1933, Hitler appointed the conservative financier Hjalmar Schacht as President of the Reichsbank. Schacht released the money necessary to expand the existing programme of state-funded projects designed to get people back to work, and by the end of the year over RM 3,000 million had been poured into it. In 1934 it consumed nearly RM 5,000 million. The money was spent on housing, public building projects, land improvement schemes, canals, bridges, railways and, most famously, Germany's network of motorways (*Autobahnen*). Between 1933 and 1938 nearly 2,000 miles of *Autobahn* roads were built.

The Nazis also expanded the existing Voluntary Labour Service scheme as a way of reducing the number of young people on the unemployment registers and providing a pool of cheap labour, mostly for agriculture. In June 1935 labour service became officially compulsory for all young Germans, although it had been so in practice since 1933. By October 1934 the number of Germans on the unemployment register had fallen to 2.2 million.

Figures 5 and 6
A propaganda photograph of Hitler at the construction of the Frankfurt to Heidelberg *Autobahn,* September 1933 (left); and a Nazi poster praising the *Autobahn* system (right).

Rearmament begins

As early as 8 February 1933 Hitler made it clear to the Cabinet 'that for the next four to five years the main principle must be: everything for the armed forces'. He also wanted the public works programme to give priority to tasks that would assist rearmament. Schacht invented a clever accounting device to achieve this. He set up a dummy holding company called Metallurgische Forschung which issued credit notes (called 'mefo' bills – an acronym of the company's name). These were given to the armaments contractors and suppliers instead of payment. They could eventually be cashed in at the Reichsbank and became, in effect, another form of currency. This system had the double advantage of stimulating Germany's depressed industrial economy by injecting much-needed money into it and of keeping secret the levels of spending on rearmament. It has been estimated that between 1934 and 1936 the mefo bills financed half of Germany's rearmament programme.

The 'New Plan' and the problems of recovery, 1934–36

Germany's economic recovery brought new problems. The construction projects needed raw materials which had to be imported from abroad. Furthermore, the newly employed workers had wages to spend which increased the demand for consumer goods and added to Germany's import bill. In the summer of 1934 Germany faced a balance of payments crisis that threatened her recovery and the progress of rearmament. Hitler responded by appointing Schacht Minister of Economics and giving him extensive powers. Schacht introduced his 'New Plan' by which importers had to seek clearance from the Economics Ministry before agreeing to buy anything abroad. This enabled the authorities to give priority to imports vital for rearmament.

The crisis of 1935–36

Schacht knew that he had not found a permanent solution to Germany's trade difficulties. As investment in rearmament became ever greater so Germany's import bill rose. Fewer goods were being produced for export because Germany's economic revival had created a profitable home market. Consumer industries and armaments firms found themselves in competition with one another for investment, raw materials and labour. As Schacht observed in 1938, 'the standard of living and the extent of armament production are in an inverse ratio'. The situation was made worse by an agricultural crisis.

Towards the end of 1935, the Nazi agricultural boss, Walther Darré, requested permission from Schacht to buy large quantities of agricultural produce abroad because German farmers were not producing enough. Schacht refused because he did not want to damage the rearmament programme which also depended on imports.

Hitler asked Göring to arbitrate and he decided in Darré's favour rather than risk unpopularity by imposing rationing. But Göring did not want to limit rearmament either. The crisis revealed the tensions and contradictions of Nazi economic policy. As Schacht had realised, it was not possible to have both 'guns and butter'. Hitler, however, believed that he could and the crisis forced him into decisive action.

Figure 7
Hitler and Hjalmar Schacht (far right) with workers building the new Reichsbank building, May 1934.

Economic policy becomes more radical

In August 1936 Hitler composed a memorandum in which he set out his ideas for solving Germany's economic problems. It is an important document because it signalled the start of a more radical period. The regime was now politically secure, its terror apparatus was firmly in place and Hitler's prestige at home and abroad was high after the successful remilitarisation of the Rhineland in March. Hitler was impatient with what he saw as the slow pace of German rearmament, especially as he was aware that his principal long-term enemy – the USSR – was rearming rapidly. He now felt he could ignore the more cautious advice of conservative figures such as Schacht. In his memorandum he demanded that 'a 100 per cent self-sufficiency should be attained in every sphere where it is feasible' regardless of cost. He concluded that 'the German armed forces must be operational within four years' and that 'the German economy must be fit for war within four years'.

The Four-Year Plan, 1936

In October 1936 Hitler gave Göring the task of carrying out these aims and he used this authority to create the Four-Year Plan Organisation, a vast bureaucratic apparatus to ensure that private industry fulfilled the aims and targets of the Plan. Before long Göring's Organisation exercised almost complete control over the allocation of investment capital, raw materials and labour. Firms, such as I. G. Farben, which co-operated with the Plan benefited from huge government contracts and investment.

Businessmen who did not co-operate faced Göring's wrath. When the heavy industrialists of the Ruhr opposed his plan for mining uneconomic ores he established a large-scale state-run industrial enterprise – the Reichswerke Hermann Göring – to compete with them. Compulsory purchase, privileged access to investment funds and plunder from the Aryanisation programme made the Reichswerke the largest industrial enterprise in Europe by 1939.

The Four-Year Plan achieved some spectacular successes. Output in most key areas was increased, and in some quite dramatically (see Key Reference,

Table 4 on page 47), but this is not surprising given that between 1936 and 1939 two-thirds of all investment went into war-related industries and that by 1939 a quarter of Germany's labour force was employed in work geared to re-armament. The Plan might have come closer to its targets had the regime been able to determine its priorities. Hitler continued to worry that a significant fall in living standards would damage his popularity. This meant that consumer production had to be maintained at tolerable levels. Precious resources were also devoted to prestige projects such as Party buildings and a new art gallery for Munich.

The Four-Year Plan typifies the Nazis' approach to government in general and to running the economy in particular. They had no grand plan to replace capitalism with a new system of fascist economics, and businessmen who co-operated with the regime grew rich. But the creation of the Reichswerke shows that the Nazis were ruthless in using their monopoly of state power to defeat opposition.

It was also typical of Hitler that he did not appoint Göring as Minister of Economics but allowed him to use the Four-Year Plan Organisation to drain power and influence away from Schacht and the Economics Ministry. Schacht opposed the policies of the Four-Year Plan because more money was being spent on producing low-quality raw materials just because they were German than it would cost to import higher-quality materials from abroad. Increasingly isolated and ignored, Schacht resigned from the Economics Ministry in November 1937 and was replaced by an ineffective Nazi called Walther Funk. In January 1939 Schacht was dismissed as President of the Reichsbank as well.

The economy and the outbreak of war

There is no doubt that the German economy was not fully mobilised for war in 1939. Some historians attribute this to deliberate policy on Hitler's part. They argue that he intended a series of short wars of plunder, each of which would allow for a period of consolidation and recovery before the next one. Such a strategy would enable living standards to be maintained because the armed forces would only require sufficient weapons for short *Blitzkrieg* (lightning war) campaigns of about six weeks at a time.

This view has been challenged. 'Total war, not blitzkrieg, was the end product of German preparations,' writes historian Richard Overy, who argues that Germany was not ready for war in 1939 because Hitler and Göring had failed to clarify their economic priorities. The nation was caught between producing armaments for an immediate war and building up the industrial infrastructure for a long war. Overy points to Hitler's grand plans, announced in 1939, for expanding the air force and the navy as evidence of his intention to fight a major war of conquest against the USSR and the British Empire in the mid-1940s. Hitler found himself at war earlier than he had intended because in 1939 he miscalculated the reaction of Britain and France to his expansionist plans.

There is a third important interpretation of the link between the state of the German economy and the timing of the outbreak of war. Tim Mason has suggested that economic crisis and the fear of popular unrest drove Hitler into a war of conquest earlier than he intended. He agrees with Overy that Hitler misjudged British policy in the Polish crisis but attributes this to Hitler's 'concern with the urgency of domestic and economic problems'. There is clear evidence of crisis in 1939: crucial sectors of the economy experienced shortages and bottlenecks, inflationary pressures were building up, skilled labour was in short supply and living standards had begun to fall. But few historians accept the Mason thesis because, despite the problems, there were no signs of serious domestic unrest in 1939. This does not entirely invalidate Mason's argument because Hitler may well have feared domestic unrest even if it did not exist. There is no doubt that Hitler was sensitive to popular opinion, but the stringent economic policies imposed once the war had begun suggest that his expansionist, aggressive instincts took priority.

Who benefited and who suffered from Nazi economic policy?

1. The middle classes

Middle-class Germans had voted for the NSDAP in the early 1930s in large numbers but their reaction to the economic policies of the Third Reich was mixed. The Nazis did little to help small businesses apart from a few cosmetic measures such as banning department stores from offering hairdressing services. Hitler was well aware that his expansionist foreign policy aims could be served only by a large-scale modern industrial economy, so he clamped down on the radicals in his party who wanted to break up the department stores and create an economy dominated by shopkeepers and small-scale manufacturers.

Most middle-class Germans welcomed the general economic improvement of the 1930s and some small businesses profited as suppliers and sub-contractors to the armaments industry or from patronage from the KdF programme (see page 27). The Aryanisation programme enabled some retailers and small businessmen to take over their Jewish rivals.

But the middle classes also resented increased state interference, higher taxes and compulsory donations to the Party. Many small businesses found themselves short of raw materials and labour once the Four-Year Plan got going. The experience of the Bavarian wooden-clog industry in 1937 was typical: it had more orders than ever before, but was unable to fulfil them because there was a shortage of leather, which prevented the straps from being made.

2. The farmers

The depressed state of German agriculture had provided the Nazis with a rich harvest of votes before 1933 and the central place of the German peasant in Nazi ideology suggested that agricultural policies would receive a high priority. Walther Darré, the Reich Peasant Leader, believed that the peasantry would provide Germany with its new Aryan aristocracy, so in September 1933 he issued the Reich Entail Farm Law. This was designed to preserve for ever Germany's medium-sized farms by preventing them from being sold or getting into debt. It was not particularly popular because such farmers were not allowed to mortgage their farms to raise money for expansion or modernisation.

Darré also established the Reich Food Estate in 1933 to control the price and distribution of agricultural produce. This huge bureaucracy was disliked by the farmers but was part of Darré's attempt to make Germany self-sufficient in agriculture. Despite a 'Battle for Production' launched in 1934, German agriculture remained dependent on imports. It also suffered from a growing labour shortage as workers left the countryside to get jobs in Germany's expanding industrial sector. Between 1933 and 1939 1.5 million workers were lost to agriculture. A milkmaid who advertised her services in a newspaper in 1939 received 130 job offers.

Because the demands of rearmament took priority, the Nazis failed to solve the problems of German agriculture, which remained under-capitalised and labour-intensive. The labour shortage alienated peasant support, which was further eroded by Nazi ideological measures and regulation.

3. The industrial working class

Workers benefited from the fall in unemployment but many of the new jobs were poorly paid and working conditions on the motorway sites were often primitive. Those who earned higher wages usually did so because they were made to work harder.

The abolition of trade unions and the regime's increasingly strict regulation of the labour market increased working-class hostility but the most common grievances were low wages and poor housing. Skilled workers were able to exploit the labour shortage of the late 1930s to improve their wages but living standards for the majority of the workforce dropped in the 1930s. Consumption of beer – always a good measure of consumer affluence – fell by 60%. Subsidised holidays and leisure pursuits were available but workers could not afford the most desirable KdF benefits. Nazi efforts to bring all Germans together in a *Volksgemeinschaft* (people's community) had more to do with propaganda than reality. Strikes, indiscipline, absenteeism and petty acts of industrial sabotage were regular occurrences, despite Nazi surveillance.

4. The industrial and business community

As with the middle classes, the reaction of the industrial and business community to the Nazis was mixed. Most employers welcomed the destruction of trade unions and the generous system of welfare established in the Weimar Republic. The power of the industrial giants such as Krupp, Siemens and Thyssen grew considerably because they benefited from the rearmament boom. Some also took advantage of the Nazis' Aryanisation programme to buy out Jewish rivals at knock-down prices. Businesses involved in exports, or in importing consumer goods, found life much tougher and most industrialists resented the increasing interference and regulation imposed by the Nazis.

The extent to which German industry was regulated has been summed up by historians Jeremy Noakes and Geoffrey Pridham: 'The Government dictated to a large extent what and how much they should produce, the amount of new investment, where new plants should be built, the type and amount of raw materials to be used, what prices to charge their customers and what wages to pay their employees, the amount of profit they could take and how it should be used – largely in reinvestment or for the purchase of Government bonds' (*Nazism*, 1919–1945).

When Hitler remarked, 'I give the orders', he summed up both the benefits and drawbacks of Nazi rule for the business and industrial community.

How successful was Nazi management of the German economy?

At first glance, the achievements of the Nazis are impressive. Unemployment was virtually eliminated by 1935, the balance of payments was stabilised, impressive roads were built, industrial output was increased and inflation was low. But on closer examination these achievements do not amount to much. Compared both to other periods of German history and to other countries in the same period, German economic growth was poor in the 1930s (see Tables 5 and 6 on page 47). The Nazis were fortunate to come to power just as the worst of the Depression was over, and were able to take the credit for an economic up-turn that would have occurred naturally whoever had been in control at the time.

Nazi policies helped to get men back to work, but by removing from the unemployment statistics those on part-time or temporary work and the young people dragooned into labour service, the government was able to make the figures look more impressive than they really were. The Nazis impeded what might have been a stronger and more lasting recovery by their emphasis on rearmament because they prevented the expansion of exports and restricted consumer demand. The Four-Year Plan distorted the economy by increasing state intervention in the capital and labour markets. Stringent controls were necessary to keep inflation in check although even these failed to prevent strikes, bottlenecks and wage increases to skilled workers from 1936 onwards. The crisis of 1939 clearly shows that the Nazis were demanding more of the German economy than it could deliver, making a war of plunder the only way of resolving the problems. And yet the Nazis' own mismanagement meant that Germany was ill-prepared even for the war that Hitler had always known was the end-product of his economic plans.

Studying 'Nazi economic policies'

1 Preparing for war was the central aim of Nazi economic policy. To understand this topic fully, you need to look at Hitler's foreign policy as well. Make a timeline with two columns, one for events in foreign policy, the other for events in economic policy. This will enable you to see how decisions and events in one area affected the other.

2 Write brief definitions of the following concepts and terms:
- *Wehrwirtschaft*
- work creation schemes
- mefo bills
- the New Plan;
- the Reich Food Estate
- the Entail Farm Law
- the Four-Year Plan
- Aryanisation (see also Chapter 5)
- *Blitzkrieg* war.

4 Consent and opposition

How far did the German people co-operate with the Nazi state, and how strong was opposition to it?

Key points

- The People's Community
- The Churches and the Third Reich
- The regime and the armed forces
- Popularity and resistance

The People's Community

The National Socialists took the 'socialism' of their title seriously. They aimed to create a national 'People's Community' (*Volksgemeinschaft*) in which class distinctions would disappear and all Germans would be united in common selfless purpose behind their *Führer*. They believed that, to be strong enough to regain Germany's rightful place in the world, the *Volksgemeinschaft* would have to remove anyone who did not conform. This meant those of inferior race and any Germans the Nazis regarded as racially unfit or ideologically unsound.

For Hitler, the Army offered the ideal model for society. This was not just because he wanted the 'whole nation in the mental state of absolute military commitment and preparedness'. He also wanted Germany to be a hierarchical society in which everyone had a valued place but unquestioningly obeyed orders from above; a society in which promotion depended on talent, drive and the ability to succeed in life's struggle, rather than on birth, class or money.

'Beauty of Labour' and 'Strength through Joy'

By November 1933 the German Labour Front (DAF), led by Robert Ley, had replaced Germany's free trade unions. Ley established two organisations within the DAF which, although principally designed to win working-class support for the regime, were also attempts to put Nazi socialism into practice. 'Beauty of Labour' campaigned for better factory working conditions although the improvements that did occur may have had as much to do with the labour shortage after 1936 (as firms competed for skilled workers) as with Ley's campaign.

The 'Strength through Joy' movement (*Kraft durch Freude* – KdF) had a dual purpose – to bring even the workers' leisure time under the regime's control, and to make what had hitherto been luxury items, such as cars or foreign holidays, available to ordinary people. Physical exercise at work became compulsory for young people, competitions were introduced to encourage productivity, and propaganda constantly stressed the nobility and community value of manual labour.

The subsidised KdF holidays were undoubtedly popular. Although few workers could afford the prestige events such as foreign cruise trips, they could take advantage of cheap railway fares, country holidays, weekend excursions, theatre trips and sports courses. Even a staunch socialist was forced to admit, 'Almost all national comrades rate KdF as one of National Socialism's really creditable achievements.'

On 26 May 1938 Hitler laid the foundation stone for the *Volkswagen* car factory at Fallersleben, near Brunswick. The aim was to produce a 'people's car' affordable by 'every German, without distinction of class, profession or property'. More than 330,000 people invested RM 280 million in the special savings scheme for those who wanted to buy one, but the factory was switched to war production in 1940 and no cars were produced until 1946.

Like the *Volkswagen*, the Nazis' aim of creating a classless society did not get very far because Hitler regarded fighting the war and destroying his racial enemies as more important. Nazi economic policies reinforced Germany's capitalist social structure and had a greater impact on German society than the KdF.

The Churches and the Third Reich

In June 1941 Hitler's private secretary, Martin Bormann, declared, 'National Socialism and Christianity are irreconcilable.' Hitler shared Bormann's convictions but his approach was always pragmatic. Christianity was too strongly entrenched in Germany to be uprooted quickly. In 1933 more than 95% of Germans were Christian, approximately two-thirds of them Protestants and one-third Roman Catholics. The Party's 1920 programme claiming that the Nazis stood for 'positive Christianity' proved enormously useful in winning the support of churchgoers before 1933, especially in the fight against the atheist communists. Once in power, Hitler had occasionally to intervene and restrain hotheads in his Party whose anti-Christian zeal provoked protest. He was well aware of the ability of the Churches to mobilise public opinion and had no intention of alienating a major source of conservative support for the regime.

The Protestant Churches

Germany's Protestants had a long tradition of conservative nationalism so many of them welcomed the Nazis' destruction of the Weimar Republic, which they saw as liberal and decadent. Even if they had wanted to resist, their internal divisions would have made it difficult. Not only were there three main Protestant groups (Lutheran, Reformed and United) but there was a small and determined set of Nazis called 'German Christians' who regarded themselves as 'the SA of the Church' and wanted to create a national church with a centralised constitution under the control of a Reich Bishop. In July 1933, after massive propaganda and a good deal of pressure, their leader, Ludwig Müller, was elected Reich Bishop.

At a rally in November, the German Christians demanded radical changes to Christian beliefs. Christ was to become a 'heroic figure' and the Jewish Old Testament was to be removed from the Bible. This provoked opposition. Led by Martin Niemöller, a group of Protestant pastors formed an 'Emergency League' to defend their faith against the German Christians. In October 1934 they formally left the Reich Church and set up a separate 'Confessional Church' which enjoyed considerable support. The arrest of two leading Lutheran bishops early in October provoked such popular uproar that Hitler intervened to have them reinstated.

Müller's attempt to gain control of the Protestant Churches and Nazify them had clearly failed and in 1935 Hitler abandoned him and created a Reich Church Ministry under Hans Kerrl, who turned out to be not much more successful than Müller. A stalemate developed. The Nazis continued to harass individuals and to challenge the Churches for control of education and youth movements, but neither side relished the prospect of a major showdown.

The Roman Catholic Church

The Roman Catholic Church was a much more formidable opponent. In the words of historian Ian Kershaw, the German Catholics possessed 'an extraordinary degree of inner strength, cohesion, unity and vitality'. The Catholic Church, unlike the Protestants, was a powerful international organisation and in Germany it possessed its own political parties – the Centre Party and its ally the Bavarian People's Party. In 1931 one of the German cardinals anticipated Bormann by declaring Nazism to be 'irreconcilable with Catholic teaching'.

Hitler knew he had to treat the Catholics with care. In contrast to the Protestants, few Catholics had voted for the NSDAP and in March 1933 Hitler needed the votes of the Centre Party and the BVP to secure the passage of the Enabling Bill. In his speech to the Reichstag on 23 March he won them over by announcing that his government 'sees in both Christian denominations the most important factors for the maintenance of our society. It will respect the agreements concluded between them and the states; their rights will not be touched.' On 28 March the Catholic bishops responded by declaring that their previously 'negative attitude' towards the Nazis 'need no longer be regarded as necessary'.

On 8 July 1933 Hitler's Roman Catholic Vice-Chancellor, Franz von Papen, successfully negotiated the Concordat between the Church and the Nazi government. The Catholics accepted the destruction of their political parties in return for freedom of worship and the independence of Catholic institutions, schools and youth clubs. Both sides were delighted with the agreement. Hitler gained international recognition and, as he told the Cabinet on 14 July, 'the permanent exclusion of the clergy from party politics . . . so much faster than I had imagined even on 30 January'. The Catholics believed that they had escaped a campaign of state persecution such as Bismarck had waged against them in the 1870s.

They were soon to be disillusioned. Radicals in the Nazi Party had no intention of respecting the Concordat and a relentless but unco-ordinated campaign began to undermine Church institutions and traditions. The SS invented Nazi rituals for birth, marriage and death. In 1938 carols and nativity plays were banned in schools and the word 'Christmas' was replaced by 'Yuletide'. Individual priests, monks and nuns were vilified in the press or arrested on charges of sexual immorality. But the most serious campaign was waged against Catholic schools, which were gradually undermined by the Nazis' tactics. Instead of banning the schools, the Nazis interfered with the curriculum, engineered the dismissal of certain teachers and abolished Christian symbols and rituals.

The Catholics resisted. In November 1936 the people of Oldenburg forced their Nazi *Gauleiter* to withdraw his ban on the display of religious symbols in public buildings and schools. The volume of protest against the arrest of a popular Munich priest in 1937 ensured that he was given only a nominal sentence. The Bavarian bishops had expressed their concern in a pastoral letter of December 1936 lamenting the 'ever-growing struggle against the Papacy'. But the same letter also indicated why Hitler could afford to ignore their protest. 'The *Führer* can be certain that we bishops are prepared to give all moral support to his historical struggle against Bolshevism. We will not criticise things which are purely political.' In March 1937 the Pope published an open letter, 'With Burning Concern', in which he condemned violations of the Concordat. It was read from all Catholic pulpits. Despite his fury, Hitler was not prepared for a head-on clash with the Church. Instead, he allowed the Nazis' campaign against Catholic individuals and institutions to intensify.

The Churches and Nazi racial policies

Both Protestants and Catholics were depressingly silent about the Nazis' racial policies. Their resistance, with the exception of some brave individuals, was confined to the defence of their own interests. Historians have debated whether the regime's barbarous policies might have been stopped if Church leaders had roundly condemned them. After all, Hitler frequently demonstrated his sensitivity to public opinion and Bishop Galen's bold sermon in August 1941 caused the suspension, officially at least, of the euthanasia campaign. On the other hand, none of the concessions given to the Churches affected issues that Hitler regarded as important. Even the euthanasia campaign was continued in secret after 1941.

Why didn't the Churches oppose the regime more strongly?

The Churches could probably have done more to obstruct Nazi policies – towards themselves and others. They did not do so because they agreed with some of Hitler's policies, especially his anti-communism. Even one of the fiercest Catholic critics of the Nazis described the war against the USSR as 'truly a crusade, a holy war for homeland and people, for faith and Church, for Christ and His most holy Cross'. Strongly nationalist Christians also tended to be anti-Semitic, describing the Jews as 'Christ-killers'. The Churches did not defend themselves more strongly because they never faced an all-out assault as the communists and socialists did. The relentless but piecemeal Nazi campaign gradually eroded their self-confidence and prevented united opposition.

The regime and the armed forces

The leaders of Germany's armed forces gave a cautious welcome to Hitler's accession to power in 1933. They shared his dislike of the Republic and were pleased that he intended to rearm and reassert Germany's power in Europe. On the other hand, some were contemptuous of his lowly origins, disliked the Party's commitment to socialism and feared the ambitions of the SA. But the knowledge that a general – Werner von Blomberg – was to be Defence Minister helped to calm their nerves.

On 3 February, Hitler spoke to a number of Army commanders at a dinner. He told them of his intention to destroy German democracy and root out communism, but reassured them that the Army would 'stay unpolitical and impartial' and that he intended 'no fusion of the Army and the SA'. He promised the reintroduction of conscription and a 'battle against Versailles'. During 1933 the Army stood by while the Nazis destroyed the left-wing parties and dismantled the constitution, but the generals became alarmed by Röhm's ambitions and his threat of a second revolution (see Chapter 1).

The Nazification of the Army

The Army played a supporting role in the 'Night of the Long Knives' in June 1934. They supplied transport and weapons for the SS men who did the actual shooting, and placed units on alert to prevent any SA resistance to the purge. More significantly, the Army's leaders turned a blind eye to the SS murder of two generals, neither of whom had anything to do with the SA. In return for Hitler's worthless promise that the Army would be 'the sole bearer of arms' in Germany, the generals agreed to a new oath of loyalty to Hitler personally.

Blomberg was convinced that 'the officer corps of the *Wehrmacht* [the German armed forces] can only fulfil its task of leadership in the nation and State if it adopts the National Socialist ideology'. In February 1934 he not only persuaded Hindenburg to allow the Nazi swastika to be worn on service uniforms but ordered the armed forces to purge their ranks of 'non-Aryans' who had not fought in the First World War. In 1935 all Jews were expelled from the forces.

Rearmament and Hitler's purge, 1938

On 9 March 1935 Hitler announced the existence of a German air force (*Luftwaffe*) and a week later issued a decree reintroducing conscription and ordering the immediate expansion of the German Army to 550,000 men – all contrary to the Versailles Treaty. Building up the German Navy was always less important to Hitler but he did sanction the construction of four battleships and, in 1937, increased this to 10. In 1939 he approved the so-called Z Plan for the creation of a large battle fleet, to be ready for action in the mid-1940s. Conscription increased the number of enthusiastic young Nazis in the armed forces and helped Blomberg's policy of making them pliant servants of the regime.

The remilitarisation the Rhineland in March 1936 delighted the generals (despite their worries beforehand) because it closed the major gap in Germany's defences. It also enormously enhanced Hitler's prestige and made resistance to his plans more difficult for the leaders of the armed forces.

By the autumn of 1937 Germany's ever-increasing rearmament programme was running into difficulties. The armed forces were competing for scarce resources with one another and with the regime's other economic objectives. But this spurred Hitler into accelerating his plans for conquest, rather than limiting them. He held a secret conference of his top military chiefs on 5 November 1937 at which he outlined his expansionist aims. Three of those present – Foreign Minister von Neurath, Army commander von Fritsch and Defence Minister von Blomberg – were worried that Hitler would drag Germany into a war before her military preparations were complete. Their reservations made Hitler determined to replace them.

Early in 1938 Hitler took advantage of a couple of scandals to be rid of Blomberg and Fritsch. Police evidence was produced that Blomberg's new young wife had been a prostitute. At the same time, the *Gestapo* dug out of its archives a file, dating back to 1936, on a male prostitute who claimed (falsely, as it turned out) to have been blackmailing Fritsch. On 4 February Hitler announced that Blomberg and Fritsch had resigned 'for reasons of health'. Von Neurath was sacked on the same day and Hitler also used the occasion to retire 16 older generals and transfer 44 more.

Hitler abolished the War Ministry and replaced it with the High Command of the Armed Forces (OKW) headed by General Keitel, whose reluctance to criticise Hitler earned him the nickname of 'the rubber lion'. The new Army commander was General Brauchitsch, who proved to be as servile as Keitel. Hitler, in the words of historian J. C. Fest, 'had thus eliminated the last power factor of any significance'.

Beck's conspiracy

There was one last attempt at military resistance before Hitler plunged Germany into war. In the summer of 1938 a few officers, led by General Beck, the Chief of the General Staff, became worried that Hitler's handling of the Czech crisis would involve Germany in a European war that 'will in all probability end not only in a military but also in a general catastrophe for Germany'. Beck hoped that a declaration of war by Britain and France in support of Czechoslovakia would encourage his fellow generals to overthrow Hitler but he failed to win the backing of Brauchitsch and resigned as Chief of Staff in August. Although Hitler's bloodless triumph at Munich in September ended the conspirators' hopes, Beck's group formed the nucleus of the resistance movement that carried out the 'bomb plot' of July 1944.

Popularity and resistance

The Hitler myth

Goebbels' propaganda machine successfully created an image of Hitler as a lonely bachelor sacrificing himself to the herculean task of rebuilding Germany and restoring her place in the world. As a result Hitler's personal popularity remained high and he was given the credit for the regime's apparently spectacular triumphs. As one German wrote, recalling his youth, 'We were living in great times, and their creator and guarantor was Hitler. Adolf Hitler, for us, was the impressive *Führer* figure. We took the picture we were given for the man. This did not prevent us from mimicking the stereotyped openings of his speeches, as a joke. But we awaited each speech with the tingling expectation that he was about to announce a new German success. We were seldom disappointed.'

The *Führer* was seen as standing above the greed and corruption of his Party officials, which explains why many who disliked the regime retained their faith in him. A socialist in Bavaria in 1938 summed up a typical attitude: 'People trust that Hitler will come one of these days and bump off Weber [a Nazi official in Munich] and the other big-shots just as he once bumped off Röhm.' Hitler remained popular until the war was obviously lost, but disillusionment with the regime, and with the Nazi Party in particular, set in much earlier.

Discontent

There is plenty of evidence that people found life in the Third Reich irksome.

Economic grievances were common, but so they are in most countries at most times. In Germany, where there was no legitimate way to protest, discontent had to be expressed through actions such as sabotage, strikes, absenteeism and graffiti-writing. Although strikes were illegal, 192 were officially recorded between February 1936 and July 1937. The actual figure was probably much higher.

The Nazis courted unpopularity when they attacked cherished traditions and institutions such as church schools, but the speed of their retreat in the face of popular protest demonstrates their sensitivity to public opinion. However, very little of this discontent posed any serious challenge to the power and legitimacy of the regime.

Terror, propaganda, participation and popularity

Despite Hitler's worries about his popularity, there was never any serious danger of the Nazi regime being overthrown from within. The terror system, even though it inspired fear and loathing, ensured that opposition was dangerous and difficult to organise. The ability of the *Gestapo* to operate outside the law, the absence of any redress and the sheer brutality of life in the concentration camps were highly effective in discouraging potential opponents. Recent research has stressed the degree to which the German people co-operated with the *Gestapo* in policing themselves (see Table 3 on page 47).

The terror system was reinforced by propaganda. Events such as the burning of the books and the exhibition in Munich in 1937 of art the Nazis considered degenerate were threats as well as propaganda displays. Ritual affirmations of faith, such as the substitution of 'Heil Hitler' for 'good morning', ensured outward conformity, at least.

Participation also encouraged co-operation. The ever-increasing involvement of the state in all aspects of life increased the number of people whose livelihoods and careers depended on the regime. Finally, much that the Nazis did was undeniably popular. Economic recovery and the destruction of the Treaty of Versailles won Hitler support from all social classes. The Nazis tapped into a number of middle-class prejudices, which meant that, at least until the war, their policies had a broad measure of consent. The crushing of the left in 1933–34, the campaign to sweep away the decadence of Weimar culture and the rounding-up of homosexuals, gypsies and vagrants all appealed to those Germans who believed in family values and the traditional virtues of cleanliness, discipline and loyalty.

Studying 'Consent and opposition'

1 List in two columns the advantages and disadvantages of life in the Third Reich for each of the following groups: workers (see also Chapter 3); Protestants; Roman Catholics; the armed forces.

2 How important was the terror system in preventing opposition to the Third Reich? Was it more or less important than other factors?

3 'Hitler was more popular than the Nazi Party.' Identify the reasons for this.

5 Nazi racial policies, 1933–39

What were the Nazis' racial beliefs and how were they translated into the persecution of minorities?

Key points

- What were the Nazis' racial theories?
- The Jewish 'problem' in Germany in 1933
- The Nuremberg Laws, 1935
- The persecution of minorities
- The radicalisation of anti-Semitism
- The SS and Jewish policy

What were the Nazis' racial theories?

Theories of race were central to Nazi ideology. The Nazis believed that the peoples of the world formed a hierarchy. At the top were the Aryans – the races of northern Europe. At the bottom were those of mixed or adulterated blood, including the Slavs of eastern Europe, gypsies and, worst of all, the Jews. Naturally, the Nazis regarded the Germans as the principal Aryan race (the master race or *Herrenvolk*), the only people capable of true civilisation, creativity and culture. They believed they were engaged in a life-and-death struggle for survival with the inferior races (*Untermenschen*).

Linked to Nazi racial theories was their belief in eugenics – the idea that all human characteristics are inherited and that selective breeding is necessary to ensure the survival of the best and eliminate the weak or undesirable. The Nazis rejected the idea that individuals have rights. 'In National Socialism the individual does not count as far as society is concerned,' said one Nazi theorist. What mattered was 'the wellbeing of the community'. These ideas explain why the Nazis felt it was their duty to purge Germany, not only of racial enemies such as Jews, but also of criminals, the insane, homosexuals and other undesirables.

The origins of Nazi anti-Semitism

The Nazis did not invent anti-Semitism. For centuries Christian countries had persecuted Jews. Government-sponsored anti-Jewish riots were common in 19th-century Russia and the Dreyfus Case in the 1890s showed the strength of anti-Semitism in France. In the late 19th century right-wing thinkers distorted Darwin's theory of evolution and invented 'Social Darwinism' – a theory that human society was composed of stronger and weaker races engaged in a struggle for survival. Hitler was influenced by these ideas during his idle teenage years in Vienna before the First World War.

Hitler's Mein Kampf

In his book, *Mein Kampf* (My Struggle), Hitler explained why he regarded the Jews as responsible for Germany's troubles. The Jews, he said, were parasites because they had never had a state of their own and had pretended to be merely a religious group rather than a race in order to become part of whatever country they lived in. This, he insisted, was their 'first and greatest lie'. In the 19th century they had grown rich as capitalism spread and they had exploited liberal democracy to gain citizenship and equal rights. These developments, he argued, were part of their plan to undermine and destroy true German culture and values. Not content with that, they had invented Marxism in an attempt to win the support of the masses. The Russian Revolution of 1917 had given them their first success. According to Hitler, Germany was defeated in 1918 not on the battlefield, but by the Jews, who had for years been 'robbing our people of the political and moral instincts and forces which alone make nations capable and hence worthy of existence'.

The appeal of anti-Semitism

Anti-Semitism did not win the Nazis many votes. Large numbers of Germans voted for the NSDAP between 1930 and 1933, not because they disliked Jews, but because they believed that only Hitler could solve Germany's severe economic and political crisis. But anti-Semitism was important to the thousands of Party activists for whom the Jews were a simple scapegoat – an enemy on whom they could blame all their troubles. In Nazi propaganda, the true German, ruined by capitalism and democracy on the one hand, and fearful of communism on the other, could see Jews at work manipulating both his enemies.

The Jewish 'problem' in Germany in 1933

There were relatively few Jews in Germany – only 500,000 in 1933, forming a mere 0.76% of the population. However, they were concentrated in certain areas. Approximately 70% lived in Germany's big cities and, compared with their representation in the population as a whole, there were significant numbers of Jews in law, medicine, commerce and the media.

Although hatred of the Jews was central to his thinking, Hitler had no clear anti-Jewish policy when he came to power in January 1933. His immediate priorities were to secure his dictatorship and get the German economy moving again. Severe measures against the Jews would hinder both these objectives because his conservative allies would object to them and economic recovery would be disrupted by attacks on Jewish businesses.

SA terror and the April boycott

Nazi activists did not share Hitler's scruples about upsetting the conservatives and went straight to work terrorising individual Jews, damaging synagogues and organising boycotts of Jewish businesses and professions. As Hitler wanted to claim that he had restored law and order in Germany, he could not tolerate such actions, however much he might sympathise with them. But he realised that he could not continue to deny his Party members their desire for some anti-Jewish measures. He decided on a nationwide boycott of Jewish

Figure 8
'Germans beware! Don't buy from Jews.' An SA member posting warning notices on a Jewish-owned shop during the 1 April 1933 boycott.

businesses and professions to begin on 1 April. This could be presented to his conservative allies as a response to what the Nazis claimed was Jewish-inspired, anti-German propaganda in the foreign press. The boycott was originally intended to last indefinitely, but, under pressure from influential conservatives in the government, Hitler restricted it to a single day.

Reactions to the boycott were mixed. In some places there was violence, in others it merely continued what the SA had been doing anyway. The response of the German public was generally apathetic and some people continued to patronise Jewish businesses in defiance of the pickets. Despite claiming the boycott a success, the Nazi leaders were aware that it had not received the public support they had hoped for.

The anti-Jewish legislation of 1933

The government also introduced some discriminatory legislation. On 7 April the Law for the Restoration of the Civil Service and the Law Concerning Admission to the Legal Profession forced 'non-Aryans' out of these professions. President Hindenburg insisted that Jews who had served in the war should be exempt and Hitler did not feel able to defy him. On 22 April the Decree Regarding Physicians' Services prohibited Jewish doctors from working in the state health system although, once again, the Hindenburg clause was applied. This decree was extended to dentists in June. On 25 April the Law Against the Overcrowding of German Schools restricted the number of Jewish students in any one school or university to 5% of the total.

The April Laws, although they began the sinister process of marginalising Germany's Jews, did not have an immediately devastating effect on the Jewish community. The Hindenburg clause meant that 70% of lawyers and 75% of doctors remained in their jobs. Within a week of the civil service law the government had to announce that it applied only to the upper levels because they could not find sufficient trained replacements. But the laws were certainly not radical enough for the Party activists, who continued their campaign of indiscriminate terror.

Propaganda Minister Goebbels had already declared war on what he called

'Jewish intellectualism' by means of book-burning ceremonies in May. The creation of the Reich Chambers of Culture in September enabled him to expel Jews from the arts and media. The loss to Germany's cultural life of its talented Jews was enormous.

German Jews in 1934

The situation in Germany stabilised a little in 1934. There was hardly any discriminatory legislation and the number of Jews leaving Germany fell from 37,000 in 1933 to 23,000 in 1934. Some 10,000 Jews even returned to Germany in early 1935 because the regime's policies appeared to be fairly mild. But Jews were still subject to arbitrary terror and harassment, and to a constant stream of hostile propaganda. They were put under pressure to resign from professional organisations, clubs and societies, and notices proclaiming 'Jews not welcome' became common in public places. Also, Julius Streicher's newspaper *Der Stürmer*, which was publicly displayed, listed Jewish professionals and businesses and the names of Germans who patronised them.

The Nuremberg Laws, 1935

By 1935 Nazi Party activists were becoming frustrated by what they saw as the lack of progress in solving the 'Jewish problem'. In particular, they wanted the government to ban marriages and sex between Germans and Jews to prevent the Jews from adulterating the blood of the Aryans. Party members had been putting local marriage officials under pressure to prevent mixed marriages for some time and the SA took to parading through the streets any prostitutes who were thought to have had Jewish clients and making them carry placards proclaiming their misdeeds. In May 1935 Party branches organised another series of boycotts and a campaign of violent terror which continued sporadically for four months.

Hitler decided it was time for action. Two days before the annual Party rally in Nuremberg was due to end, he ordered his Interior Minister to draw up laws banning relationships between Germans and Jews.

The Nuremberg Laws were issued on 15 September 1935. The Law for the Protection of German Blood and German Honour banned marriages and sex between Germans and Jews. It also prohibited Jews from employing female German servants under 45 years of age. The Reich Citizenship Law denied Jews German citizenship. These laws were an important milestone in the isolation of Germany's Jews, who were now officially labelled as second-class. The laws were also Hitler's demonstration that, although he had been spurred into action by the activities of his Party radicals, he was determined to retain control of the pace, direction and nature of anti-Jewish policy.

These laws made it essential to define Jewishness. Nazi ideology stated that the Jews were a race and not a religion but in the 'First Supplementary Decree to the Reich Citizenship Law', promulgated on 14 November, the Nazis were forced to use membership of 'the Jewish religious community' as the basis of their definition. A Jew was someone with three or more Jewish grandparents. Those with two were classified as part-Jews (*Mischlinge* 'first degree') unless they were members of the Jewish religion, were married to a Jew or had one fully Jewish parent in which case they were regarded as full Jews. Those with only one Jewish grandparent were classified as *Mischlinge* 'second degree'.

Further discrimination soon followed. Civil servants spared by the Hindenburg clause were dismissed and Jews were banned from all state service. The courts were soon active in condemning Jews and Aryans for having sexual relations with each other, or 'race defilement' as the Nazis called it. Of the cases initiated by the *Gestapo* in the Bavarian city of Würzburg, 54% began with denunciations from German citizens. Although this is a small sample, it does suggest that Nazi anti-Jewish propaganda had begun to succeed.

The Nuremberg Laws affected Germans as well as Jews because it now became essential to have proof of Aryan ancestry. 'Genealogical researchers' made money by searching through parish records, and 'racial experts' undertook physical examinations of doubtful cases. Applicants for entry to the SS were asked for proof of Aryan ancestry dating back to 1650.

The persecution of minorities

A law issued on 14 July 1933 required those who were considered to be suffering from mental or hereditary illnesses to be compulsorily sterilised. Furthermore, the definition of hereditary diseases was widened to include chronic alcoholism and 'moral feeble-mindedness', a term so vague that the authorities could interpret it as they wished. It is estimated that between 320,000 and 350,000 people were sterilised in accordance with this law. The absence of opposition to it suggests that, in official circles at least, Nazi ideas about eugenics were accepted.

Hitler was also planning a euthanasia programme. As early as 1929 he had declared at a Party rally that: 'if Germany was to get a million children a year and was to remove 700,000 to 800,000 of the weakest people, then the final result might even be an increase in strength.' In 1935 he told Gerhard Wagner that 'in the event of war he would take up the question of euthanasia and enforce it', because 'such a problem would be more easily solved in wartime'. In 1938 a parent wrote to Hitler requesting a mercy killing for his deformed child. Hitler handed the issue over to the Head of his Chancellery, Philip Bouhler, who was looking for a way to extend his power. Bouhler set up a secret committee to examine all cases of deformed births and to pronounce on whether the children were to live or die. Soon after the war started, Hitler authorised Bouhler to extend his work to adults. By the time the programme was officially suspended in 1941, about 100,000 mentally ill people had been killed.

The 'work-shy', asocials and criminals

According to the Nazis, anti-social behaviour was inherited. They also believed that the criminal classes were breeding faster than healthy, respectable Germans. There were regular police raids to arrest beggars and vagrants, some of whom were designated 'feeble-minded' and compulsorily sterilised. A law of November 1933 allowed the police to retain indefinitely anyone with two or more criminal convictions. Many were subjected to 'criminal-biological' investigations by 'experts' to determine whether or not they should be castrated. In December 1937 Himmler defined the asocial as 'persons who demonstrate through behaviour towards the community . . . that they will not adapt themselves to the community'. This vague definition allowed the *Gestapo* to round up as many as 11,000 people in raids begun in April 1938 and use them as cheap labour in the concentration camps.

Homosexuals

Homosexuals were considered racial enemies by the Nazis because, in Himmler's words, they had 'renounced their duty to procreate'. They should be killed, 'just as we pull out weeds, throw them on a heap and burn them'. Homosexuality had been illegal throughout Germany since 1871 but in 1935 the Nazis widened the definition of criminal behaviour to include anything likely to offend 'public morality'. It is estimated that between 10,000 and 15,000 homosexuals were imprisoned in concentration camps during the Third Reich.

Gypsies

As nomads without regular jobs or settled homes, gypsies had been subject to official hostility before 1933. To the Nazis, they were both the 'carriers of alien blood' and work-shy asocials with criminal tendencies. They were subjected to the Nazis' racial laws, many were arrested in the police round-ups of vagrants and some were sterilised while in custody. In 1936 they become the special interest of Dr Robert Ritter's research unit. He wanted to separate what he thought was the minority of pure Aryan gypsies from the part-gypsies who were believed to be the carriers of criminal characteristics and especially dangerous because of their inter-breeding with Germans. In December 1938 Himmler's 'Decree for the Struggle against the Gypsy Nuisance' gave SS support to Ritter's attempts to create a systematic register of all gypsies. Himmler's aims were 'the physical separation of Gypsydom from the German nation' and 'the regulation of the way of life of pure and part-Gypsies'. Gypsies became confined to designated sites and, after Germany's victory over Poland in 1939, many were transported east. Ritter's plan to keep his 'pure Aryan' gypsies in a kind of human zoo was overruled by Hitler and after 1941 500,000 of Europe's gypsies became victims of the Holocaust.

Anti-Semitism becomes more radical

Aryanisation

With the attention of the world focused on the Berlin Olympics, 1936 was a relatively quiet year for Germany's Jews. But by the autumn of 1937 Hitler had decided to begin a more extreme phase in Nazi policy. Göring, who had been put in charge of a Four-Year Plan to prepare Germany's economy for war, turned his attention to those Jews who still exercised economic power and began his programme of 'Aryanisation'. This involved buying out Jewish firms or confiscating Jewish economic assets. Up till then, major Jewish businesses had remained untouched because the Nazis had wanted their co-operation in the economic recovery and the rearmament programme.

A good deal of Aryanisation of small businesses had occurred since 1933; possibly as many as 75,000 Jewish firms were liquidated in the first two years of Nazi rule. This was part of the almost continual campaign of local terror and harassment. Customers who used Jewish shops were photographed and intimidated, Jewish shopkeepers were prosecuted for minor violations of the law and Aryan clients refused to pay their debts. Even so, the Nazis themselves estimated that there were still nearly 40,000 Jewish businesses in Germany in April 1938.

Backed by Göring, German capitalists were able to buy out their major Jewish rivals, often at bargain prices. The process was not always straightforward since some Jewish firms had Aryan shareholders, others were parts of large conglomerates and some had major assets abroad. Göring assisted in December 1937 by reducing the foreign exchange and raw materials quotas for Jewish firms and, in March 1938, by banning Jewish firms from receiving government contracts. When the seizure of Austria increased the number of Jewish firms to be plundered, Göring issued a 'Decree for the Registration of Jewish Property' in April 1938 by which all Jewish assets worth more than RM 5,000 had to be registered and could not be sold or leased without government permission.

Other measures to isolate Germany's Jews followed. In March 1938 Jewish religious congregations were deprived of legal protection and in June Jewish doctors were banned from treating Aryan patients. This was followed by a similar measure against lawyers, dentists and vets. Jews were also banned from certain commercial occupations. On 17 July all Jews were required to adopt an additional first name, 'Israel' for men, and 'Sarah' for women.

'Kristallnacht', *9–10 November 1938*

The intensity of the government's campaign against the Jews in 1938 encouraged a new wave of intimidation and terror by Party activists, which culminated in the notorious 'Night of Broken Glass' (*Kristallnacht*). On 7 November 1938, a Jewish youth shot and killed a German embassy official in Paris in revenge for the Nazis' treatment of his parents. Propaganda Minister Josef Goebbels seized on the event as an opportunity to regain Hitler's favour after the *Führer* had ordered him to end his affair with a Czech actress. He got Hitler to agree that 'the SA should be allowed to have its final fling' and instructed Party members to carry out 'demonstrations' against the Jewish community in Germany during the night of 9–10 November. These would be presented to the outside world as the 'spontaneous' reaction of the German people to the Paris murder.

In an unprecedented orgy of violence, 8,000 Jewish shops and homes were attacked, most synagogues set on fire, about 100 Jews killed and more than 20,000 arrested.

The event shocked the outside world. Many Germans, too, were horrified but there were few protests. Göring, however, was furious. He had wanted to plunder Jewish property, not destroy it and he resented Goebbels' interference. On Hitler's orders Göring summoned a conference of the Nazi top brass on 12 November to co-ordinate policy towards the Jews. In a typically callous move, Göring announced that the Jews were to be fined RM 1 billion for the damage caused on Crystal Night and that any payments they received from insurance claims would be confiscated by the Reich. A decree was issued formally excluding Jews from economic activity. This allowed the Aryanisation programme to be accelerated.

One of those who attended Göring's conference was Himmler's SS deputy, Reinhard Heydrich. He pointed out that, 'because of Aryanising and other restrictions, Jewry will become unemployed . . . I shall therefore have to take steps to isolate the Jew so that he won't enter into the normal German routine of life.' Heydrich proposed that Jews should be made to wear a badge of identification. Although this was not implemented until 1941, Heydrich's contribution to the conference indicated that Jewish policy was increasingly to be a police matter, controlled not by Göring, but by the SS.

The SS and Jewish policy

As the self-styled racial élite of Nazi Germany, the SS had always taken an interest in the Jewish question, but until 1936 Himmler's principal concern was to secure his position as Germany's chief of police. In 1934 the SS had produced a secret 'Situation Report – Jewish Question' for Himmler which advocated Jewish emigration. They distinguished between Zionist Jews who wanted to live in Palestine and those who wished to remain because they considered themselves Germans. The former should be encouraged, and the latter persecuted. In 1936 the SS set up their own Jewish department and began to gather detailed records of Germany's Jews. As ever, the SS adopted a bureaucratic and systematic approach to the problem in contrast to the amateur, violent and arbitrary methods of other Party agencies.

SS attempts at encouraging emigration were not particularly successful: only a minority of German Jews were Zionists and the British restricted the numbers of Jews settling in Palestine. SS policy also clashed with Göring's Aryanisation because Jews were not welcome abroad without their economic assets.

Immediately after the Anschluss with Austria, the SS Jewish expert, Adolf Eichmann, established a 'Central Office for Jewish Emigration' in Vienna. The incorporation of Austria had added 200,000 Jews to Germany's total. Eichmann followed a ruthless policy of compulsory emigration. Jewish assets were either seized or used to finance the emigration. Within six months, he had forced out a quarter of Austria's Jews. Such was his success that in February 1939 a Reich Central Office for Jewish Emigration was established in Berlin. The SS also set up a Reich Association for the Jews in Germany to co-ordinate all Jewish organisations and assist in the preparations for emigration.

When the war broke out, the SS were in complete control of Nazi Jewish policy. But the war made emigration impractical. Instead it drove the Nazis into 'the final solution of the Jewish question' which Hitler had hinted at in his Reichstag speech in January 1939: 'If the international Jewish financiers in and outside Europe should succeed in plunging the nations once more into a world war, then the result will not be the Bolshevizing of the world, and thus the victory of Jewry, but the annihilation of the Jewish race in Europe.'

Studying 'Nazi racial policies'

1 Make a timeline of the important events of Nazi anti-Semitic policy. Compare it with your timeline on foreign and economic policies. Can you identify any common trends?

2 How much did Hitler and his government control racial policy and to what extent were they pushed into action by the radicals in the Nazi Party? Identify on your timeline the events you believe were: **a)** initiated by Hitler, **b)** caused by pressure or action by the radicals.

3 Make notes on the key factors which enabled the SS to dominate racial policy by the time the war broke out. Your notes should include the following points:
- SS control of the police and terror system (see also Chapter 2)
- their systematic approach to racial policy
- their control of the other aspects of racial policy, apart from anti-Semitism
- Eichmann's emigration policy
- the effect of Nazi policies becoming progressively more extreme.

6 Interpreting the Third Reich

Historical interpretations of Nazi Germany and Hitler's role

Key points

- Totalitarianism and Fascism
- Reactionary or revolutionary?
- Was the Third Reich an aberration or a product of German history?
- Can Nazism be described as Hitlerism?

Totalitarianism and fascism

At the height of the Cold War it was fashionable to compare the USSR and its eastern European satellites with the fascist regimes of the 1930s – Italy and Nazi Germany in particular. They were all regarded as examples of totalitarian states.

What were the features of the totalitarian states of the 1930s?

- The state aimed to control every aspect of life – hence the word 'totalitarian'. Everyone had to subscribe to the aims, values and ideas of the official ideology. No one had a 'private' life because the government aimed to control even such personal matters as a person's thoughts or sexual activity.
- The state was led by a dictator whose word was law. His rule was enforced by an extensive terror system and a single political party that monopolised all positions of power.
- The economy was closely directed by the state and workers had no rights or bargaining power.
- Tight censorship of the press and all forms of culture ensured that only official views were expressed. Traditional values such as patriotism, the importance of family life and obedience to authority were constantly stressed while the education system and a state-controlled youth movement were used to indoctrinate the next generation.
- Totalitarian leaders regarded their people, not as a collection of individuals, but as a single united body. They believed that people only mattered in so far as they served the common purpose; those who did not had to be purged lest they contaminate others.

Was the Third Reich a totalitarian state?

All of the features mentioned above applied to Nazi Germany and Stalinist Russia and most of them to Fascist Italy. However, in recent years, many historians have discarded the concept of totalitarianism because it obscures the chaotic and unplanned way in which decisions were reached and masks too many of the crucial differences between the three countries.

Was the Third Reich a Fascist state?

From 1936 onwards, Germany and Italy were allies. Both disliked and opposed communism as well as the liberal, capitalist democracies of the west. But Mussolini's control was never as total as Hitler's. He lacked many of the Nazis' most radical ambitions, in particular, their fanatical and barbarous racial policies. Modern historians of the Third Reich regard it as unique.

Reactionary or revolutionary?

To Soviet historians the Nazis were the reactionary tools of German capitalists who brought Hitler to power and used him for their own purposes. This interpretation did not survive the collapse of communism. A more sophisticated Marxist analysis was offered by Tim Mason (*Social Policy in the Third Reich*, 1993), who argued that Hitler's links with the capitalist and reactionary classes were crucial to his rise to power but that he escaped their control once in office.

Recent scholarship has placed much more emphasis on the Nazis' racial policies. Although there were many reactionary elements to Nazism – in particular, as regards cultural values – the cosmic scope of their barbaric racial vision makes Nazism undoubtedly revolutionary (Burleigh and Wippermann, *The Racial State*, 1991).

Was the Third Reich an aberration or a product of German history?

Were the Nazis a bunch of criminals who hijacked the German state and carried out their destructive policies without the active co-operation of the German people? Or does the Third Reich show that there is some flaw in the German character? Argument on this issue has been fierce because it raises serious questions about the responsibility of the whole German nation for such terrible events as the Second World War and the Holocaust.

There are intellectual heavyweights on both sides. Gordon Craig believes that the arguments used 'to prove Hitler's kinship with other German statesmen or to demonstrate the native roots of his political behaviour are too trivial to be persuasive. Adolf Hitler was *sui generis*, a force without a real historical past . . . He stands alone' (*Germany*, 1866–1945, 1978). But Hitler's principal German biographer, J. C. Fest, believes that Nazism was a product (though not an inevitable one) of 'a long and wretched tradition of German intellectual history' (*Hitler*, 1973).

The debate has recently been given added impetus by the work of historians who have analysed the extent to which ordinary Germans co-operated with the *Gestapo* in policing themselves and with the SS in carrying out the

Holocaust. Even 50 years after Hitler's fall, the issue of German 'guilt' causes controversy (Gellately, *The Gestapo and German Society*, 1990; Goldhagen, *Hitler's Willing Executioners*, 1996).

Can Nazism be described as Hitlerism?

Did Hitler decide everything?

Hitler's warped personality continues to fascinate people. Popular and scholarly biographies abound. There has even been a psycho-historical study suggesting that his troubles were caused by a missing testicle. Some of the most influential books on the Third Reich have been biographies of Hitler, notably those of Alan Bullock (*Hitler: A Study in Tyranny*, 1952) and J. C. Fest. Perhaps inevitably, his biographers have tended to regard Hitler and Nazism as one and the same.

They are supported by a distinguished group of scholars who regard Hitler's personality and ideas as central to the history of the Third Reich and who believe that he was responsible for all major policy decisions. K. D. Bracher (*The German Dictatorship*, 1971) believes that 'National Socialism can indeed be called Hitlerism'. The extraordinary similarity between what Hitler said in *Mein Kampf* that he wanted to do and the policies carried out during the Third Reich is the strongest evidence in support of this interpretation.

This approach has been criticised by other historians who argue that it does not sufficiently take account of the background against which Hitler's decisions were made. How far was he influenced by others? To what extent did the structure of German society and politics determine events? Were there individuals and groups in the Third Reich who acted autonomously? And if the Third Reich was a product of German history, can it be explained simply in terms of Hitler and his personality?

Did the system determine how decisions were made?

The foremost critic of the Hitler-centred interpretation was Martin Broszat (*The Hitler State*, 1981), who argued that Nazi Germany was polycratic – that the chaos and inefficiency of its government had created many centres of power. Unlike previous historians who believed that Hitler had deliberately created this confusion to preserve his own authority, Broszat argued that it derived from the nature of Nazism. The NSDAP before 1933 had been a conglomeration of groups and individuals all fighting for position and influence. Once in office, the structure and methods of the Party were applied to the state. Hitler was neither willing nor able to change a system in which his subordinates, anxious to increase their own power, took decisions and initiated policies independently of one another. Broszat went on to argue that Nazi policies became more extreme, not because Hitler was in control, ticking off the stages on his timetable, but because of the process of endless competition between individuals and agencies. The only way to elbow someone else out of the way was to adopt a more extreme policy. Broszat termed this process 'cumulative radicalisation'.

One of the best examples of this appears to be the issue of Nazi anti-Semitism. Despite his obsession with Jews, Hitler seemed to have had no clear idea of what he wanted to do about them and intervened only occasionally in policy-making in the 1930s. As a result, Jewish policy became a battleground between party radicals, often acting on their own authority at a local level, and Nazi barons such as Göring, Goebbels and Himmler all competing to enlarge their empires.

One historian has even concluded that Hitler was weak. Hans Mommsen has described him as 'unwilling to take decisions, frequently uncertain, exclusively concerned with upholding his prestige and personal authority, influenced in the strongest fashion by his current entourage . . . in all questions which needed the adoption of a fundamental and definitive position, a weak dictator'.

Conclusions

Both interpretations have their merits. There is plenty of evidence of in-fighting and ad hoc decision-making, but the attempt to shift Hitler to the margins is surely misguided. Equally, Hitler's ideological consistency is compelling, even if he did not control every aspect of policy and was clearly not working to a strategic timetable.

It seems likely that Hitler was perfectly happy not to interfere because the process of 'cumulative radicalisation' was taking policy where he wanted it to go. He knew that he could intervene to restrain hotheads or give things a push when he needed to. He was uninterested in many aspects of policy, which helps to explain his willingness to give his subordinates a free rein.

Hitler's reluctance to get involved in day-to-day issues left plenty of scope for others to make decisions and, like any other politician, his freedom of manoeuvre was affected by circumstances. But there is no doubt that his uniquely barren and destructive philosophy shaped the direction of Nazi policy. Without Hitler, the history of Germany would have been very different.

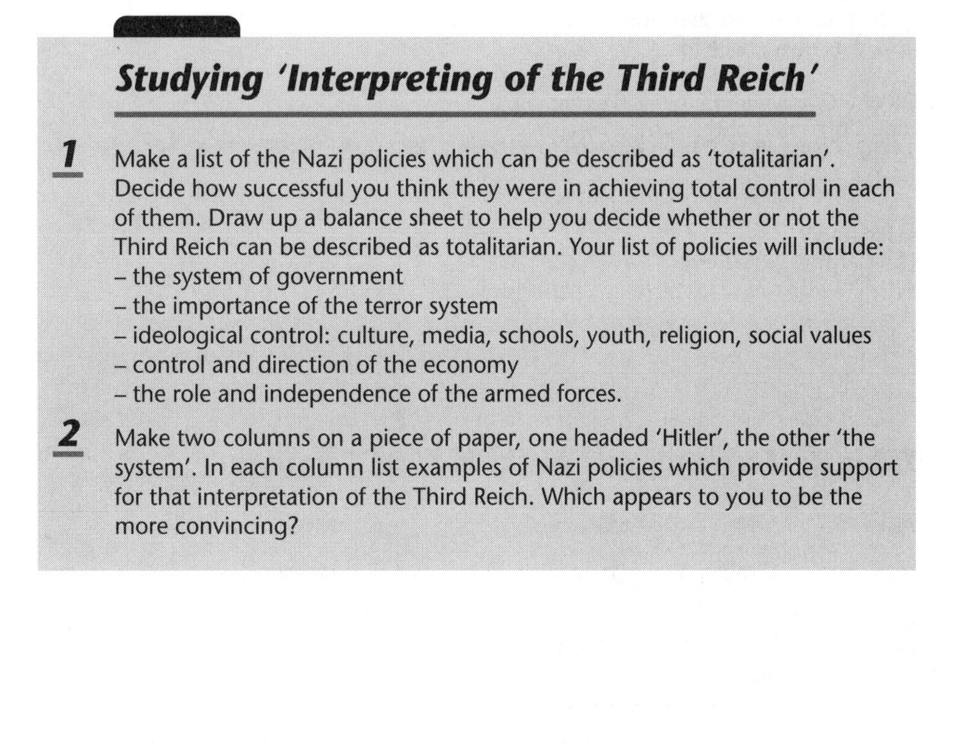

Studying 'Interpreting of the Third Reich'

1 Make a list of the Nazi policies which can be described as 'totalitarian'. Decide how successful you think they were in achieving total control in each of them. Draw up a balance sheet to help you decide whether or not the Third Reich can be described as totalitarian. Your list of policies will include:
- the system of government
- the importance of the terror system
- ideological control: culture, media, schools, youth, religion, social values
- control and direction of the economy
- the role and independence of the armed forces.

2 Make two columns on a piece of paper, one headed 'Hitler', the other 'the system'. In each column list examples of Nazi policies which provide support for that interpretation of the Third Reich. Which appears to you to be the more convincing?

Table 1: Glossary of terms

Blitzkrieg
'Lightning war': a strategy of short but swift attacks designed to paralyse enemy forces.

Concentration camps
Initially makeshift prisons set up by the SA. In 1934 the camps were taken over by the SS and run with brutal efficiency.

DAF – *Deutsche Arbeitsfront*
The German Labour Front: the Nazi trade union to which all workers belonged.

Gauleiter
A Nazi regional leader, responsible directly to Hitler.

Gestapo
An abbreviation of *Geheime Staatspolizei* (Secret State Police). Set up by Göring in Prussia in 1933, it came under the control of Himmler and the SS in 1934. It was responsible for surveillance throughout Germany.

Herrenvolk
The master race.

Länder
Germany's regional states. There were 17 in 1933. Each had its own government and parliament and controlled its own police force.

OKW – *Oberkommando der Wehrmacht*
High Command of the Armed Forces, established in 1938 when Hitler abolished the War Ministry.

Reichstag
The German Parliament.

SA – *Sturmabteilung*
The 'storm section' of the Nazi Party. Founded in 1921, it was the Party's paramilitary force used to intimidate political opponents.

SD – *Sicherheitsdienst*
The Security Service of the SS. Founded in 1932, it became the intelligence branch of the SS.

SS – *Schutzstaffel*
Originally Hitler's bodyguard, or 'guard unit', it grew into the Nazi police force or Reich Protection Corps.

Untermenschen
The inferior people. A term used by the Nazis to identify the races that would serve the master race or be exterminated.

Volksgemeinschaft
The 'people's community' based on race, not class.

Wehrwirtschaft
Defence economy: the idea that all the nation's resources should be prepared in peacetime for war.

Table 2: Marriages and births in Nazi Germany

Year	Marriages	Births
1932	516,793	971,174
1934	740,165	1,198,350
1936	609,770	1,278,583
1938	645,062	1,348,534

1938 figures include territories taken over by Germany in 1938

(From T. Kirk, *The Longman Companion to Nazi Germany*, 1995)

Table 3: Co-operation of the German people with the Gestapo in Düsseldorf

The reason the *Gestapo* began an investigation	Number	Percentage
Reports from the population	213	26
Information from other control organisations	139	17
Observation by Düsseldorf *Gestapo* agents	127	15
Information from state or local authorities	57	7
Statements at interrogation	110	13
Information from businesses	24	3
Information from Nazi organisation	52	6
No information	103	13
Total	825	100

(From R. Gellately, *The Gestapo and German Society*, 1990)

Table 4: The Four-Year Plan

Commodity	1936 output	1938 output	1942 output	Plan target
Mineral oil*	1,790	2,340	6,260	13,830
Aluminium	98	166	260	273
Buna rubber	0.7	5	96	120
Nitrogen	770	914	930	1,040
Explosives	18	45	300	223
Powder	20	26	150	217
Steel	19,216	22,656	20,480	24,000
Iron ore	2,255	3,360	4,137	5,549
Brown coal	161,382	194,985	245,918	240,500
Hard coal	158,400	186,186	166,059	213,000

Output measured in thousands of tons
* including synthetic petrol

(From J. Noakes and G. Pridham, *Nazism 1919–1945*)

Table 5: Economic growth of selected countries

(Gross National Product in 1937 compared to that of 1913)

USA	171.9	1913 = 100
Sweden	174.0	
Italy	154.2	
Britain	146.5	
Germany	136.4	
France	120.8	

(From R. J. Overy, *The Nazi Economic Recovery, 1932–1938*, 2nd ed., 1996)

Table 6: Average annual growth rates in Germany

	% growth
1870–1913	2.9
1913–1950	1.2
1913–1938	2.6
1950–1960	7.6
1950–1970	6.2

(From R. J. Overy, *The Nazi Economic Recovery, 1932–1938*, 2nd ed., 1996)